GERMAN
VOCABULARY

ENGLISH-GERMAN

The most useful words
To expand your lexicon and sharpen
your language skills

5000 words

German vocabulary for English speakers - 5000 words

By Andrey Taranov

T&P Books vocabularies are intended for helping you learn, memorize and review foreign words. The dictionary is divided into themes, covering all major spheres of everyday activities, business, science, culture, etc.

The process of learning words using T&P Books' theme-based dictionaries gives you the following advantages:

- Correctly grouped source information predetermines success at subsequent stages of word memorization
- Availability of words derived from the same root allowing memorization of word units (rather than separate words)
- Small units of words facilitate the process of establishing associative links needed for consolidation of vocabulary
- Level of language knowledge can be estimated by the number of learned words

T&P Books Publishing
www.tpbooks.com

ISBN: 978-1-78071-319-9

This book is also available in E-book formats.
Please visit www.tpbooks.com or the major online bookstores.

GERMAN VOCABULARY
for English speakers

T&P Books vocabularies are intended to help you learn, memorize, and review foreign words. The vocabulary contains over 5000 commonly used words arranged thematically.

- Vocabulary contains the most commonly used words
- Recommended as an addition to any language course
- Meets the needs of beginners and advanced learners of foreign languages
- Convenient for daily use, revision sessions, and self-testing activities
- Allows you to assess your vocabulary

Special features of the vocabulary

- Words are organized according to their meaning, not alphabetically
- Words are presented in three columns to facilitate the reviewing and self-testing processes
- Words in groups are divided into small blocks to facilitate the learning process
- The vocabulary offers a convenient and simple transcription of each foreign word

The vocabulary has 155 topics including:

Basic Concepts, Numbers, Colors, Months, Seasons, Units of Measurement, Clothing & Accessories, Food & Nutrition, Restaurant, Family Members, Relatives, Character, Feelings, Emotions, Diseases, City, Town, Sightseeing, Shopping, Money, House, Home, Office, Working in the Office, Import & Export, Marketing, Job Search, Sports, Education, Computer, Internet, Tools, Nature, Countries, Nationalities and more ...

T&P BOOKS' THEME-BASED DICTIONARIES

The Correct System for Memorizing Foreign Words

Acquiring vocabulary is one of the most important elements of learning a foreign language, because words allow us to express our thoughts, ask questions, and provide answers. An inadequate vocabulary can impede communication with a foreigner and make it difficult to understand a book or movie well.

The pace of activity in all spheres of modern life, including the learning of modern languages, has increased. Today, we need to memorize large amounts of information (grammar rules, foreign words, etc.) within a short period. However, this does not need to be difficult. All you need to do is to choose the right training materials, learn a few special techniques, and develop your individual training system.

Having a system is critical to the process of language learning. Many people fail to succeed in this regard; they cannot master a foreign language because they fail to follow a system comprised of selecting materials, organizing lessons, arranging new words to be learned, and so on. The lack of a system causes confusion and eventually, lowers self-confidence.

T&P Books' theme-based dictionaries can be included in the list of elements needed for creating an effective system for learning foreign words. These dictionaries were specially developed for learning purposes and are meant to help students effectively memorize words and expand their vocabulary.

Generally speaking, the process of learning words consists of three main elements:

- Reception (creation or acquisition) of a training material, such as a word list
- Work aimed at memorizing new words
- Work aimed at reviewing the learned words, such as self-testing

All three elements are equally important since they determine the quality of work and the final result. All three processes require certain skills and a well-thought-out approach.

New words are often encountered quite randomly when learning a foreign language and it may be difficult to include them all in a unified list. As a result, these words remain written on scraps of paper, in book margins, textbooks, and so on. In order to systematize such words, we have to create and continually update a "book of new words." A paper notebook, a netbook, or a tablet PC can be used for these purposes.

This "book of new words" will be your personal, unique list of words. However, it will only contain the words that you came across during the learning process. For example, you might have written down the words "Sunday," "Tuesday," and "Friday." However, there are additional words for days of the week, for example, "Saturday," that are missing, and your list of words would be incomplete. Using a theme dictionary, in addition to the "book of new words," is a reasonable solution to this problem.

The theme-based dictionary may serve as the basis for expanding your vocabulary.

It will be your big "book of new words" containing the most frequently used words of a foreign language already included. There are quite a few theme-based dictionaries available, and you should ensure that you make the right choice in order to get the maximum benefit from your purchase.

Therefore, we suggest using theme-based dictionaries from T&P Books Publishing as an aid to learning foreign words. Our books are specially developed for effective use in the sphere of vocabulary systematization, expansion and review.

Theme-based dictionaries are not a magical solution to learning new words. However, they can serve as your main database to aid foreign-language acquisition. Apart from theme dictionaries, you can have copybooks for writing down new words, flash cards, glossaries for various texts, as well as other resources; however, a good theme dictionary will always remain your primary collection of words.

T&P Books' theme-based dictionaries are specialty books that contain the most frequently used words in a language.

The main characteristic of such dictionaries is the division of words into themes. For example, the *City* theme contains the words "street," "crossroads," "square," "fountain," and so on. The *Talking* theme might contain words like "to talk," "to ask," "question," and "answer".

All the words in a theme are divided into smaller units, each comprising 3–5 words. Such an arrangement improves the perception of words and makes the learning process less tiresome. Each unit contains a selection of words with similar meanings or identical roots. This allows you to learn words in small groups and establish other associative links that have a positive effect on memorization.

The words on each page are placed in three columns: a word in your native language, its translation, and its transcription. Such positioning allows for the use of techniques for effective memorization. After closing the translation column, you can flip through and review foreign words, and vice versa. "This is an easy and convenient method of review – one that we recommend you do often."

Our theme-based dictionaries contain transcriptions for all the foreign words. Unfortunately, none of the existing transcriptions are able to convey the exact nuances of foreign pronunciation. That is why we recommend using the transcriptions only as a supplementary learning aid. Correct pronunciation can only be acquired with the help of sound. Therefore our collection includes audio theme-based dictionaries.

The process of learning words using T&P Books' theme-based dictionaries gives you the following advantages:

* You have correctly grouped source information, which predetermines your success at subsequent stages of word memorization
* Availability of words derived from the same root (lazy, lazily, lazybones), allowing you to memorize word units instead of separate words
* Small units of words facilitate the process of establishing associative links needed for consolidation of vocabulary
* You can estimate the number of learned words and hence your level of language knowledge
* The dictionary allows for the creation of an effective and high-quality revision process
* You can revise certain themes several times, modifying the revision methods and techniques
* Audio versions of the dictionaries help you to work out the pronunciation of words and develop your skills of auditory word perception

The T&P Books' theme-based dictionaries are offered in several variants differing in the number of words: 1.500, 3.000, 5.000, 7.000, and 9.000 words. There are also dictionaries containing 15,000 words for some language combinations. Your choice of dictionary will depend on your knowledge level and goals.

We sincerely believe that our dictionaries will become your trusty assistant in learning foreign languages and will allow you to easily acquire the necessary vocabulary.

TABLE OF CONTENTS

PRONUNCIATION GUIDE

Letter	German example	T&P phonetic alphabet	English example

Vowels

a	da, das	[a]	shorter than in ask
e	Erde, eschreiben	[ɛ]	man, bad
e	halte	[ə]	driver, teacher
i	ihr, finden	[ɪ]	big, America
o	wohnen, oft	[ɔ]	bottle, doctor
u	Schule, dumm	[u], [ʊ]	noodles, mango
y [1]	Pony	[i]	shorter than in feet
y [2]	Gymnastik	[y]	fuel, tuna
ä	hängen	[ɛ:]	longer than bed, fell
ö	Öl, zwölf	[ø:]	first, thirsty
ü	über, dünn	[y:]	longer than fuel

Consonants

b	baden	[b]	baby, book
b [3]	Abschied	[p]	pencil, private
d	dunkel	[d]	day, doctor
d [4]	Abend	[t]	tourist, trip
f	fünf	[f]	face, food
g	gelb	[g]	game, gold
g [5]	Tag	[k]	clock, kiss
g [6]	lustig	[h]	huge, humor
g [7]	Ingenieur	[ʒ]	forge, pleasure
h [8]	heute	[h]	home, have
h	Sohn	[h]	silent [h]
j [9]	Journalist	[ʒ]	forge, pleasure
j [10]	ja	[j]	yes, New York
k	Küche	[k]	clock, kiss
l	loben	[l]	lace, people
m	Morgen	[m]	magic, milk

Letter	German example	T&P phonetic alphabet	English example
n	Name	[n]	name, normal
p	Papier	[p]	pencil, private
r	richtig	[r]	rice, radio
s [11]	sein	[z]	zebra, please
s [12]	Spielzeug	[ʃ]	machine, shark
s [13]	Haus (n)	[s]	city, boss
ß	weiß	[s]	city, boss
v [14]	November	[v]	very, river
v [15]	Vater	[f]	face, food
w	was	[w]	vase, winter
x	Axt	[ks]	box, taxi
z	Zeit	[z]	zebra, please

Combinations of letters

ch [16]	auch	[h]	home, have
ch [17]	Chaos	[k]	clock, kiss
ch [18]	Chance	[ʃ]	machine, shark
ch [19]	ich	[ɦ]	huge, humor
chs	wachsen	[ks]	box, taxi
ck	backen	[k]	clock, kiss
dt	Stadt	[t]	tourist, trip
ng	Zeitung	[ŋ]	English, ring
nk	Bank	[ŋk]	bank, trunk
ph	Philosophie	[f]	face, food
qu	Quelle	[kv]	square, quality
sch	Schalter	[ʃ]	machine, shark
th	Thema	[t]	tourist, trip
tsch	Deutsch	[ʧ]	church, French
tz	Netz	[ʦ]	cats, tsetse fly

Vowels and diphthongs

er	Hunger	[ə]	driver, teacher

Diphthongs

ei, ey	Seite	[aɪ]	tie, driver
au	auch	[aʊ]	now, down
äu	Gebäude	[ɔɪ]	oil, boy, point
eu	neu	[ɔɪ]	oil, boy, point

Comments

[1] in loanwords
[2] elsewhere
[3] at the end of a word
[4] at the end of a word
[5] at the end of a word
[6] in the suffix -ig
[7] in loanwords
[8] at the beginning of a word
[9] in loanwords
[10] elsewhere
[11] before a vowel
[12] in sp
[13] elsewhere
[14] in loanwords
[15] elsewhere
[16] after a, o, u, au
[17] in Greek loanwords
[18] in French loanwords
[19] elsewhere

ABBREVIATIONS
used in the vocabulary

ab.	-	about
adj	-	adjective
adv	-	adverb
anim.	-	animate
as adj	-	attributive noun used as adjective
e.g.	-	for example
etc.	-	et cetera
fam.	-	familiar
fem.	-	feminine
form.	-	formal
inanim.	-	inanimate
masc.	-	masculine
math	-	mathematics
mil.	-	military
n	-	noun
pl	-	plural
pron.	-	pronoun
sb	-	somebody
sing.	-	singular
sth	-	something
v aux	-	auxiliary verb
vi	-	intransitive verb
vi, vt	-	intransitive, transitive verb
vt	-	transitive verb

m, f	-	masculine, feminine
m	-	masculine noun
f	-	feminine noun
m pl	-	masculine plural
f pl	-	feminine plural
n pl	-	neuter plural
m, n	-	masculine, neuter
f, n	-	feminine, neuter
mod	-	modal verb

BASIC CONCEPTS

Basic concepts. Part 1

1. Pronouns

I, me	ich	[iħ]
you	du	[dʊ]
he	er	[ɛr]
she	sie	[zi:]
it	es	[ɛs]
we	wir	[wi:r]
you (to a group)	ihr	[i:r]
you (polite, sing.)	Sie	[zi:]
you (polite, pl)	Sie	[zi:]
they	sie	[zi:]

2. Greetings. Salutations. Farewells

Hello! (fam.)	**Hallo!**	[ha'lø:]
Hello! (form.)	**Hallo!**	[ha'lø:]
Good morning!	**Guten Morgen!**	['gʊːtn 'mɔrgn]
Good afternoon!	**Guten Tag!**	['gʊːtn 'tak]
Good evening!	**Guten Abend!**	['gʊːtn 'abnt]
to say hello	**grüßen** (vi, vt)	['gry:sən]
Hi! (hello)	**Hallo!**	[ha'lø:]
greeting (n)	**Gruß** (m)	[grʊ:s]
to greet (vt)	**begrüßen** (vt)	['bəgrysən]
How are you?	**Wie geht's?**	[wi 'ge:t əs]
What's new?	**Was gibt es Neues?**	[vas gipt əs 'nɔjes]
Bye-Bye! Goodbye!	**Auf Wiedersehen!**	['auf 'wi:dərze:ən]
See you soon!	**Bis bald!**	[bis balt]
Farewell! (to a friend)	**Lebe wohl!**	['le:bə vɔ:l]
Farewell (form.)	**Leben Sie wohl!**	['le:bən zi: vɔl]
to say goodbye	**sich verabschieden**	[ziħ fɛrap'ʃi:dən]
So long!	**Tschüs!**	[ʧus]
Thank you!	**Danke!**	['daŋkə]
Thank you very much!	**Dankeschön!**	['daŋkə 'ʃɔn]

You're welcome	**Bitte!**	['bitə]
Don't mention it!	**Keine Ursache!**	['kaınə 'u:zahə]
It was nothing	**Nichts zu danken!**	[niħʦ ʦu 'daŋkən]
Excuse me! (fam.)	**Entschuldige!**	[ɛnt'ʃʊldigə]
Excuse me! (form.)	**Entschuldigung!**	[ɛnt'ʃʊldigʊŋ]
to excuse (forgive)	**entschuldigen** (vt)	[ɛnt'ʃʊldigən]
to apologize (vi)	**sich entschuldigen**	[ziħ ɛnt'ʃʊldigən]
My apologies	**Verzeihung!**	[fɛr'ʦajuŋ]
I'm sorry!	**Entschuldigung!**	[ɛnt'ʃʊldigʊŋ]
to forgive (vt)	**verzeihen** (vt)	[fɛr'ʦaıən]
It's okay!	**Das macht nichts!**	[dɑs maħt niħʦ]
please (adv)	**bitte**	['bitə]
Don't forget!	**Nicht vergessen!**	[niħt fɛr'gɛsən]
Certainly!	**Natürlich!**	[na'tyrliħ]
Of course not!	**Natürlich nicht!**	[na'tyrliħ 'niħt]
Okay! (I agree)	**Gut! Okay!**	[gʊ:t ɔ'kɛı]
That's enough!	**Es ist genug!**	[ɛs ist 'gənʊk]

3. How to address

mister, sir	**Herr**	[hɛr]
ma'am	**Frau**	['frau]
miss	**Frau**	['frau]
young man	**Junger Mann**	['juŋə man]
young man (little boy)	**Junge**	['juŋə]
miss (little girl)	**Mädchen**	['mɛ:thən]

4. Cardinal numbers. Part 1

0 zero	**null**	[nʊl]
1 one	**eins**	[aıns]
2 two	**zwei**	[ʦvaı]
3 three	**drei**	[draı]
4 four	**vier**	[fi:ə]
5 five	**fünf**	[fynf]
6 six	**sechs**	[zɛks]
7 seven	**sieben**	[zi:bn]
8 eight	**acht**	[aht]
9 nine	**neun**	[nɔın]
10 ten	**zehn**	[ʦe:n]
11 eleven	**elf**	[ɛlf]
12 twelve	**zwölf**	['ʦwølf]
13 thirteen	**dreizehn**	['draıʦe:n]
14 fourteen	**vierzehn**	['firʦe:n]

15 fifteen	fünfzehn	['fynftse:n]
16 sixteen	sechzehn	['zɛhtsə:n]
17 seventeen	siebzehn	['zi:ptse:n]
18 eighteen	achtzehn	['ahtsəin]
19 nineteen	neunzehn	['nɔɪntse:n]

20 twenty	zwanzig	['tsvantsifi]
21 twenty-one	einundzwanzig	['aɪn unt 'tsvantsifi]
22 twenty-two	zweiundzwanzig	['tsvaɪ unt 'tsvantsifi]
23 twenty-three	dreiundzwanzig	['draɪ unt 'tsvantsifi]

30 thirty	dreißig	['draɪsifi]
31 thirty-one	einunddreißig	['aɪn unt 'draɪsifi]
32 thirty-two	zweiunddreißig	['tsvaɪ unt 'draɪsifi]
33 thirty-three	dreiunddreißig	['draɪ unt 'draɪsifi]

40 forty	vierzig	['firtsifi]
41 forty-one	einundvierzig	['aɪn unt 'firtsifi]
42 forty-two	zweiundvierzig	['tsvaɪ unt 'firtsifi]
43 forty-three	dreiundvierzig	['draɪ unt 'firtsifi]

50 fifty	fünfzig	['fynftsifi]
51 fifty-one	einundfünfzig	['aɪn unt 'fynftsifi]
52 fifty-two	zweiundfünfzig	['tsvaɪ unt 'fynftsifi]
53 fifty-three	dreiundfünfzig	['draɪ unt 'fynftsifi]

60 sixty	sechzig	['zɛhtsifi]
61 sixty-one	einundsechzig	['aɪn unt 'zɛhtsifi]
62 sixty-two	zweiundsechzig	['tsvaɪ unt 'zɛhtsifi]
63 sixty-three	dreiundsechzig	['draɪ unt 'zɛhtsifi]

70 seventy	siebzig	['zi:ptsifi]
71 seventy-one	einundsiebzig	['aɪn unt 'zi:ptsifi]
72 seventy-two	zweiundsiebzig	['tsvaɪ unt 'zi:ptsifi]
73 seventy-three	dreiundsiebzig	['draɪ unt 'zi:ptsifi]

80 eighty	achtzig	['ahtsifi]
81 eighty-one	einundachtzig	['aɪn unt 'ahtsifi]
82 eighty-two	zweiundachtzig	['tsvaɪ unt 'ahtsifi]
83 eighty-three	dreiundachtzig	['draɪ unt 'ahtsifi]

90 ninety	neunzig	['nɔɪntsifi]
91 ninety-one	einundneunzig	['aɪn unt 'nɔɪntsifi]
92 ninety-two	zweiundneunzig	['tsvaɪ unt 'nɔɪntsifi]
93 ninety-three	dreiundneunzig	['draɪ unt 'nɔɪntsifi]

5. Cardinal numbers. Part 2

| 100 one hundred | einhundert | [aɪn 'hʊndərt] |
| 200 two hundred | zweihundert | [tsvaɪ 'hʊndərt] |

300 three hundred	**dreihundert**	[draɪ 'hʊndərt]
400 four hundred	**vierhundert**	[fir 'hʊndərt]
500 five hundred	**fünfhundert**	[fynf 'hʊndərt]
600 six hundred	**sechshundert**	[zɛks 'hʊndərt]
700 seven hundred	**siebenhundert**	['ziːbn 'hʊndərt]
800 eight hundred	**achthundert**	[aht 'hʊndərt]
900 nine hundred	**neunhundert**	[nɔɪn 'hʊndərt]
1000 one thousand	**eintausend**	[aɪn 'tauzənt]
2000 two thousand	**zweitausend**	[ʦvaɪ 'tauzənt]
3000 three thousand	**dreitausend**	[draɪ 'tauzənt]
10000 ten thousand	**zehntausend**	[ʦeːn 'tauzənt]
one hundred thousand	**hunderttausend**	['hʊndərt 'tauzənt]
million	**Million** (f)	[mi'lɔn]
billion	**Milliarde** (f)	[mi'ʎjardə]

6. Ordinal numbers

first (adj)	**der erste**	[də 'ɛrstə]
second (adj)	**der zweite**	[də 'ʦvaɪtə]
third (adj)	**der dritte**	[də 'dritə]
fourth (adj)	**der vierte**	[də 'fiːrtə]
fifth (adj)	**der fünfte**	[də 'fynftə]
sixth (adj)	**der sechste**	[də 'zɛkstə]
seventh (adj)	**der siebte**	[də 'ziːptə]
eighth (adj)	**der achte**	[də 'ahtə]
ninth (adj)	**der neunte**	[də 'nɔɪntə]
tenth (adj)	**der zehnte**	[də ʦeːntə]

7. Numbers. Fractions

fraction	**Bruch** (m)	[brʊh]
one half	**Hälfte** (f)	['hɛlftə]
one third	**Drittel** (n)	['dritl]
one quarter	**Viertel** (n)	['firtəl]
one eighth	**Achtel** (n)	['ahtl]
one tenth	**Zehntel** (n)	['ʦeːntl]
two thirds	**zwei Drittel**	[ʦvaɪ 'dritl]
three quarters	**drei Viertel**	[draɪ 'fiːrtl]

8. Numbers. Basic operations

subtraction	**Subtraktion** (f)	[zuptrak'ʦʲɔːn]
to subtract (vi, vt)	**subtrahieren** (vt)	[zuptra'iːrən]

| division | Division (f) | [diwi'zʲɔːn] |
| to divide (vt) | dividieren (vt) | [diwi'diːrən] |

addition	Addition (f)	[adi'tsʲɔːn]
to add up (vt)	addieren (vt)	[a'diːrən]
to add (vi, vt)	hinzufügen (vt)	[hin'tsuːfyːgən]
multiplication	Multiplikation (f)	[mʊltiplika'tsʲɔːn]
to multiply (vt)	multiplizieren (vt)	[mʊltipli'tsiːrən]

9. Numbers. Miscellaneous

digit, figure	Ziffer (f)	['tsifə]
number	Zahl (f)	[tsaːl]
numeral	Zahlwort (n)	['tsaːlvɔrt]
minus sign	Minus (n)	['miːnʊs]
plus sign	Plus (n)	[plys]
formula	Formel (f)	['fɔrml]

calculation	Berechnung (f)	['bərɛhnʊŋ]
to count (vt)	zählen (vt)	['tsɛːlən]
to count up	berechnen (vt)	['bərɛhnən]
to compare (vt)	vergleichen (vt)	[fɛrg'laɪhn]

How much?	Wie viel?	['wiːfiːl]
How many?	Wie viele?	[wiː 'fiːlə]
sum, total	Summe (f)	['zumə]
result	Ergebnis (n)	[ɛr'geːpnis]
remainder	Rest (m)	[rɛst]

a few ...	einige	['aɪnigə]
few, little (adv)	wenig ...	['weːniɦ]
the rest	Übrige (n)	['juːbrigə]
one and a half	anderthalb	['andərthalp]
dozen	Dutzend (n)	['dʊtsənt]

in half (adv)	entzwei	[ɛntsʲvaɪ]
equally (evenly)	zu gleichen Teilen	[tsu 'glaɪhən 'taɪlən]
half	Hälfte (f)	['hɛlftə]
time (three ~s)	Mal (n)	[maːl]

10. The most important verbs. Part 1

to advise (vt)	raten (vt)	['raːtən]
to agree (say yes)	zustimmen (vi)	['tsuːʃtimən]
to answer (vi, vt)	antworten (vi)	['antvɔrtən]
to apologize (vi)	sich entschuldigen	[ziɦ ɛnt'ʃʊldigən]
to arrive (vi)	ankommen (vi)	['aŋkɔmən]
to ask (~ oneself)	fragen (vt)	['fraːgən]

to ask (~ sb to do sth)	bitten (vt)	['bitən]
to be (vi)	sein (vi)	[zaɪn]
to be afraid	Angst haben	['aŋst 'ha:bn]
to be hungry	hungrig sein	['hʊŋ rɪɦ zaɪn]
to be interested in …	sich interessieren	[zɪɦ ɪntərɛ'si:rən]
to be needed	nötig sein	['nø:tɪɦ zaɪn]
to be surprised	staunen (vi)	['ʃtaunən]
to be thirsty	Durst haben	['dʊrst ha:bn]
to begin (vt)	beginnen (vt)	['bəgɪnən]
to belong to …	gehören (vi)	['gəhø:rən]
to boast (vi)	prahlen (vi)	['pra.lən]
to break (split into pieces)	brechen (vt)	['brɛhn]
to call (for help)	rufen (vi)	['rʊ:fən]
can (v aux)	können (mod)	['kønən]
to catch (vt)	fangen (vt)	['faŋən]
to change (vt)	ändern (vt)	['ɛndərn]
to choose (select)	wählen (vt)	['vɛlən]
to come down	herabsteigen (vi)	[he'rapʃtaɪgən]
to come in (enter)	hereinkommen (vi)	[hɛ'raɪŋkɔmən]
to compare (vt)	vergleichen (vt)	[fɛrg'laɪhn]
to complain (vi, vt)	klagen (vi)	['kla:gən]
to confuse (mix up)	verwechseln (vt)	[fɛrv:'ɛksəln]
to continue (vt)	fortsetzen (vt)	['fɔrtzətsən]
to control (vt)	kontrollieren (vt)	[kɔntrɔ'li:rən]
to cook (dinner)	zubereiten (vt)	['tsu:bəraɪtən]
to cost (vt)	kosten (vt)	['kɔstən]
to count (add up)	rechnen (vt)	['rɛɦnən]
to count on …	auf … zählen	['auf 'tsɛlən]
to create (vt)	schaffen (vt)	['ʃafən]
to cry (weep)	weinen (vi)	['vaɪnən]

11. The most important verbs. Part 2

to deceive (vi, vt)	täuschen (vt)	['tɔɪʃn]
to decorate (tree, street)	schmücken (vt)	['ʃmykən]
to defend (a country, etc.)	verteidigen (vt)	[fɛr'taɪdɪgən]
to demand (request firmly)	verlangen (vt)	[fɛr'laŋən]
to dig (vt)	graben (vt)	[gra:bn]
to discuss (vt)	besprechen (vt)	['bəʃprɛhn]
to do (vt)	machen (vt)	['mahn]
to doubt (have doubts)	zweifeln (vi)	['tsvaɪfəln]
to drop (let fall)	fallen lassen	['fa:lən 'lasən]
to exist (vi)	existieren (vi)	[ɛkzis'ti:rən]

to expect (foresee)	voraussehen (vt)	[fɔ'rausze:ən]
to explain (vt)	erklären (vt)	[ɛrk'lerən]
to fall (vi)	fallen (vi)	['fa:lən]
to find (vt)	finden (vt)	['findən]
to finish (vt)	beenden (vt)	[be:'ɛndən]
to fly (vi)	fliegen (vi)	['fli:gən]
to follow ... (come after)	folgen (vi)	['fɔlgən]
to forget (vi, vt)	vergessen (vt)	[fɛr'gɛsn]
to forgive (vt)	verzeihen (vt)	[fɛr'tsaɪən]
to give (vt)	geben (vt)	[ge:bn]
to give a hint	andeuten (vt)	['andɔɪtən]
to go (on foot)	gehen (vi)	['ge:ən]
to go for a swim	schwimmen gehen	['ʃwi:mən 'ge:ən]
to go out (from ...)	ausgehen (vi)	['ausge:ən]
to guess right	richtig raten (vt)	['riɦtiɦ 'ra:tən]
to have (vt)	haben (vt)	[ha:bn]
to have breakfast	frühstücken (vi)	['fry:ʃtykən]
to have dinner	zu Abend essen	[tsu 'a:bənt 'ɛsn]
to have lunch	zu Mittag essen	[tsu 'mita:k 'ɛsn]
to hear (vt)	hören (vt)	['hø:rən]
to help (vt)	helfen (vi)	['hɛlfən]
to hide (vt)	verstecken (vt)	[fɛrʃ'tɛkən]
to hope (vi, vt)	hoffen (vi)	['hɔfən]
to hunt (vi, vt)	jagen (vi)	['jagən]
to hurry (vi)	sich beeilen	[ziɦ 'beaɪlən]

12. The most important verbs. Part 3

to inform (vt)	informieren (vt)	[infɔr'mi:rən]
to insist (vi, vt)	bestehen (vi)	['bəʃte:ən]
to insult (vt)	kränken (vt)	['krɛŋkən]
to invite (vt)	einladen (vt)	['aɪnladən]
to joke (vi)	Witz machen	[wits mahn]
to keep (vt)	aufbewahren (vt)	['aufbə'va:rən]
to keep silent	schweigen (vi)	['ʃvaɪgən]
to kill (vt)	ermorden (vt)	[ɛr'mɔrdən]
to know (sb)	kennen (vt)	['kɛnən]
to know (sth)	wissen (vt)	['wisn]
to laugh (vi)	lachen (vi)	['lahn]
to liberate (city, etc.)	befreien (vt)	['bəfraɪən]
to like (I like ...)	gefallen (vi)	['gəfalən]
to look for ... (search)	suchen (vt)	['zu:hən]
to love (sb)	lieben (vt)	[li:bn]

to make a mistake	**sich irren**	[ziɦ 'irən]
to manage, to run	**leiten** (vt)	['laɪtən]
to mean (signify)	**bedeuten** (vt)	['bədɔɪtən]
to mention (talk about)	**erwähnen** (vt)	[ɛr'vɛnən]
to miss (school, etc.)	**versäumen** (vt)	[fɛr'zɔɪmən]
to notice (see)	**bemerken** (vt)	['bəmɛrkən]
to object (vi, vt)	**einwenden** (vt)	[aɪn'vɛntən]
to observe (see)	**beobachten** (vt)	['bəobahtən]
to open (vt)	**öffnen** (vt)	[øfnən]
to order (meal, etc.)	**bestellen** (vt)	['bəʃtɛlən]
to order (mil.)	**befehlen** (vt)	['bəfeːlən]
to own (possess)	**besitzen** (vt)	[bəzɪsən]
to participate (vi)	**teilnehmen** (vi)	['taɪlneːmən]
to pay (vi, vt)	**zahlen** (vt)	['ʦaːlən]
to permit (vt)	**erlauben** (vt)	[ɛr'laubn]
to plan (vt)	**planen** (vt)	['plaːnən]
to play (children)	**spielen** (vi, vt)	['ʃpiːlən]
to pray (vi, vt)	**beten** (vi)	['beːtən]
to prefer (vt)	**vorziehen** (vt)	['foːrʦien]
to promise (vt)	**versprechen** (vt)	[fɛrʃp'rɛhn]
to pronounce (vt)	**aussprechen** (vt)	['ausʃprɛhn]
to propose (vt)	**vorschlagen** (vt)	['forʃlaːgən]
to punish (vt)	**bestrafen** (vt)	['bəʃtraːfən]
to read (vi, vt)	**lesen** (vi, vt)	['leːzn]
to recommend (vt)	**empfehlen** (vt)	[ɛmp'feːlən]
to refuse (vi, vt)	**sich weigern**	[ziɦ 'vaɪgərn]
to regret (be sorry)	**bedauern** (vt)	['bədauərn]
to rent (sth from sb)	**mieten** (vt)	['miːtən]
to repeat (say again)	**noch einmal sagen**	[nɔɦ 'aɪnmal zaːgn]
to reserve, to book	**reservieren** (vt)	[rezər'wiːrən]
to run (vi)	**laufen** (vi)	['laufən]

13. The most important verbs. Part 4

to save (rescue)	**retten** (vt)	['rɛtən]
to say (~ thank you)	**sagen** (vt)	['zaːgən]
to scold (vt)	**schelten** (vt)	['ʃɛltən]
to see (vt)	**sehen** (vi, vt)	['zeːən]
to sell (vt)	**verkaufen** (vt)	[fɛr'kaufən]
to send (vt)	**abschicken** (vt)	['apʃikən]
to shoot (vi)	**schießen** (vi)	['ʃiːsən]
to shout (vi)	**schreien** (vi)	['ʃraɪən]
to show (vt)	**zeigen** (vt)	['ʦaɪgən]
to sign (document)	**unterschreiben** (vt)	[untərʃ'raɪbn]

| to sit down (vi) | sich setzen | [ziħ 'zɛtsən] |
| to smile (vi) | lächeln (vi) | ['lɛhəln] |

to speak (vi, vt)	sprechen (vi)	['ʃprɛhn]
to steal (money, etc.)	stehlen (vt)	['ʃteːlən]
to stop (please ~ calling me)	einstellen (vt)	['aɪnʃtələn]
to stop (for pause, etc.)	stoppen (vt)	['ʃtɔpən]
to study (vt)	lernen (vt)	['lɛrnən]
to swim (vi)	schwimmen (vi)	['ʃwimən]

to take (vt)	nehmen (vt)	['neːmən]
to think (vi, vt)	denken (vi, vt)	['dɛŋkən]
to threaten (vt)	drohen (vi)	['droːən]
to touch (with hands)	berühren (vt)	['bəryːrən]
to translate (vt)	übersetzen (vt)	[juːbər'zɛtsən]
to trust (vt)	vertrauen (vi)	[fɛrt'rauən]
to try (attempt)	versuchen (vt)	[fɛr'zuːhən]
to turn (~ to the left)	abbiegen (vi)	['apbiːgən]

to underestimate (vt)	unterschätzen (vt)	[untər'ʃɛtsən]
to understand (vt)	verstehen (vt)	[fɛrʃ'teːən]
to unite (vt)	vereinigen (vt)	[fɛ'raɪnigən]

to wait (vt)	warten (vi)	['vartən]
to want (wish, desire)	wollen (vt)	['vɔlən]
to warn (vt)	warnen (vt)	['varnən]
to work (vi)	arbeiten (vi)	['arbaɪtən]
to write (vt)	schreiben (vi, vt)	[ʃraɪbn]
to write down	aufschreiben (vt)	['aufʃraɪbn]

14. Colors

color	Farbe (f)	['farbə]
shade (tint)	Schattierung (f)	[ʃa'tiːrʊŋ]
hue	Farbton (m)	['faːrbtoːn]
rainbow	Regenbogen (m)	['reːgənboːgən]

white (adj)	weiß	[vaɪs]
black (adj)	schwarz	[ʃvarts]
gray (adj)	grau	['grau]

green (adj)	grün	[gryn]
yellow (adj)	gelb	[gəlp]
red (adj)	rot	[roːt]

blue (adj)	blau	['blau]
light blue (adj)	hellblau	['hɛlblau]
pink (adj)	rosa	['roːza]
orange (adj)	orange	[ɔ'ranʒ]

violet (adj)	**violett**	[wɪɔ'let]
brown (adj)	**braun**	['braun]
golden (adj)	**golden**	['gɔldən]
silvery (adj)	**silbrig**	['zilbriɦ]
beige (adj)	**beige**	[be:ʒ]
cream (adj)	**cremefarben**	['krɛːmfarbn]
turquoise (adj)	**türkis**	['tyrkiːs]
cherry red (adj)	**kirschrot**	['kirʃrɔːt]
lilac (adj)	**lila**	['liːla]
crimson (adj)	**himbeerrot**	[himbeːɐr'rɔt]
light (adj)	**hell**	[hɛl]
dark (adj)	**dunkel**	['dʊŋkl]
bright, vivid (adj)	**grell**	[grəl]
colored (pencils)	**Farb-**	['farp]
color (e.g., ~ film)	**Farb-**	['farp]
black-and-white (adj)	**schwarz-weiß**	['ʃvartsvaɪs]
plain (one-colored)	**einfarbig**	['aɪnfarbiɦ]
multicolored (adj)	**bunt**	[bʊnt]

15. Questions

Who?	**Wer?**	[we:r]
What?	**Was?**	[vas]
Where? (at, in)	**Wo?**	[vɔ:]
Where (to)?	**Wohin?**	[vɔ:'hin]
From where?	**Woher?**	[vɔ:'he:r]
When?	**Wann?**	[van]
Why? (What for?)	**Wozu?**	[vɔ:'ʦu:]
Why? (reason)	**Warum?**	[va'rʊm]
What for?	**Wofür?**	[vɔ:'fy:r]
How? (in what way)	**Wie?**	[wi:]
What? (What kind of ...?)	**Welcher?**	['vɛlhə]
Which?	**Welcher?**	['vɛlhə]
To whom?	**Wem?**	[we:m]
About whom?	**Über wen?**	[ju:bə vɛ:n]
About what?	**Wovon?**	[vɔ:'fon]
With whom?	**Mit wem?**	[mit we:m]
How many?	**Wie viele?**	[wi: 'fi:lə]
How much?	**Wie viel?**	['wi:fi:l]
Whose?	**Wessen?**	['vɛsn]

16. Prepositions

with (accompanied by)	mit	[mit]
without	ohne	['ɔːnə]
to (indicating direction)	nach	[naːh]
about (talking ~ ...)	über	['juːbə]
before (in time)	vor	[foːr]
in front of ...	vor	[foːr]
under (beneath, below)	unter	['untə]
above (over)	über	['juːbə]
on (atop)	auf	['auf]
from (off, out of)	aus	['aus]
of (made from)	aus, von	['aus], [fɔn]
in (e.g., ~ ten minutes)	in	[in]
over (across the top of)	über	['juːbə]

17. Function words. Adverbs. Part 1

Where? (at, in)	Wo?	[vɔː]
here (adv)	hier	[hiːə]
there (adv)	dort	[dɔrt]
somewhere (to be)	irgendwo	['irgəntvɔː]
nowhere (not anywhere)	nirgends	['nirgənts]
by (near, beside)	an	[an]
by the window	am Fenster	[am 'fɛnstə]
Where (to)?	Wohin?	[vɔː'hin]
here (e.g., come ~!)	hierher	['hiːrheːr]
there (e.g., to go ~)	dahin	[da'hin]
from here (adv)	von hier	[fɔn hiːə]
from there (adv)	von da	[fɔn daː]
close (adv)	nah	[naː]
far (adv)	weit	[vait]
near (e.g., ~ Paris)	in der Nähe von ...	[in də 'nɛːə fɔn]
nearby (adv)	in der Nähe	[in də 'nɛːə]
not far (adv)	unweit	[unvait]
left (adj)	link	[liŋk]
on the left	links	[liŋks]
to the left	nach links	[naːh 'liŋks]
right (adj)	recht	[rɛht]
on the right	rechts	[rɛhts]

to the right	nach rechts	[naːh ˈrɛçts]
in front (adv)	vorne	[ˈfɔrnə]
front (as adj)	Vorder-	[ˈfɔrdə]
ahead (look ~)	vorwärts	[ˈfɔːrvɛrts]

behind (adv)	hinten	[ˈhintən]
from behind	von hinten	[fɔn ˈhintən]
back (towards the rear)	rückwärts	[ˈrykvɛrts]

| middle | Mitte (f) | [ˈmitə] |
| in the middle | in der Mitte | [in də ˈmitə] |

⬛ ⬛⬛ ⬛⬛⬛	⬛⬛⬛⬛⬛⬛	[ˈⱫ⬛⬛⬛⬛]
everywhere (adv)	überall	[ˈjuːbə ˈal]
around (in all directions)	ringsherum	[riŋshəˈrʊm]

from inside	von innen	[fɔn ˈinən]
somewhere (to go)	irgendwohin	[ˈirgəntvɔːhin]
straight (directly)	geradeaus	[ˈgəraːdəaʊs]
back (e.g., come ~)	zurück	[tsuˈryk]

| from anywhere | irgendwoher | [ˈirgəntvɔheː] |
| from somewhere | von irgendwo | [fɔn ˈiːgəntvʊ] |

firstly (adv)	erstens	[ˈɛrstəns]
secondly (adv)	zweitens	[ˈtsvaɪtəns]
thirdly (adv)	drittens	[ˈdritəns]

suddenly (adv)	plötzlich	[ˈpløtsliç]
at first (adv)	zuerst	[tsuˈɛrst]
for the first time	zum ersten Mal	[tsum ˈɛrstən ˈmaːl]
long before ...	lange vor ...	[ˈlaŋə fɔr]
anew (over again)	von Anfang an	[fɔn ˈanfaŋ an]
for good (adv)	für immer	[fyːr ˈimə]

never (adv)	nie	[ni]
again (adv)	wieder	[ˈwiːdə]
now (adv)	jetzt	[jetst]
often (adv)	oft	[ɔft]
then (adv)	damals	[ˈdaːmaːls]
urgently (quickly)	dringend	[ˈdriŋənt]
usually (adv)	gewöhnlich	[ˈgəwøːnliç]

by the way, ...	übrigens, ...	[ˈjuːbrigəns]
possible (that is ~)	möglicherweise	[møklihəˈvaɪzə]
probably (adv)	wahrscheinlich	[vaːrˈʃaɪnliç]
maybe (adv)	vielleicht	[fiˈlaɪçt]
besides ...	außerdem ...	[ˈausərdəm]
that's why ...	deshalb ...	[ˈdɛsˈhalp]
in spite of ...	trotz ...	[trɔts]
thanks to ...	dank ...	[daŋk]
what (pron.)	was	[vas]

that (conj.)	das	[das]
something	etwas	['ɛtvas]
anything (something)	irgendwas	['irgəntvas]
nothing	nichts	[niħts]

who (pron.)	wer	[we:r]
someone	jemand	['jemant]
somebody	irgendwer	['irgəntwe:r]

nobody	niemand	['ni:mant]
nowhere (a voyage to ~)	nirgends	['nirgənts]
nobody's	niemandes	['ni:mandəs]
somebody's	jemandes	['jemandəs]

so (I'm ~ glad)	so	[zɔ:]
also (as well)	auch	['auh]
too (as well)	ebenfalls	['e:bənfals]

18. Function words. Adverbs. Part 2

Why?	Warum?	[va'rʊm]
for some reason	aus irgendeinem Grund	['aus ju:gntaınəm g'ry:nt]
because ...	weil ...	[vaıl]
for some purpose	zu irgendeinem Zweck	[ʦu i:gən'taınəm ʦvɛk]

and	und	[unt]
or	oder	['ɔ:də]
but	aber	['a:bə]
for (e.g., ~ me)	für	[fy:r]

too (~ many people)	zu	[ʦu:]
only (exclusively)	nur	[nʊ:r]
exactly (adv)	genau	['gənau]
about (more or less)	etwa	['ɛtva]

approximately (adv)	ungefähr	['uŋ əfə:r]
approximate (adj)	ungefähr	['uŋ əfə:r]
almost (adv)	fast	[fast]
the rest	Übrige (n)	['ju:brigə]

other (different)	andere	['andərə]
each (adj)	jeder (m)	['je:də]
any (no matter which)	beliebig	['bəli:biħ]
many, much (a lot of)	viel	[fi:l]
many people	viele Menschen	['file mɛnʃən]
all (everyone)	alle	['alə]

| in return for ... | im Austausch gegen ... | [im 'austauʃ 'ge:gn] |
| in exchange (adv) | dafür | ['dafyə] |

by hand (made)	mit der Hand	[mit də hant]
hardly (negative opinion)	schwerlich	['ʃweːrliħ]
probably (adv)	wahrscheinlich	[vaːrˈʃaɪnliħ]
on purpose (adv)	absichtlich	['apziħtliħ]
by accident (adv)	zufällig	['ʦufɛliħ]
very (adv)	sehr	[zeːr]
for example (adv)	zum Beispiel	[ʦum ˈbaɪʃpiːl]
between	zwischen	['ʦwiʃn]
among	unter	['untə]
so much (such a lot)	so viel	[▮▮▮ ▮▮.▮]
▮▮▮▮▮ ▮▮▮▮▮ ▮▮▮ ▮	besonders	['bezɔndərs]

Basic concepts. Part 2

19. Weekdays

Monday	**Montag** (m)	['mɔ:nta:k]
Tuesday	**Dienstag** (m)	['di:nsta:k]
Wednesday	**Mittwoch** (m)	['mitvɔh]
Thursday	**Donnerstag** (m)	['dɔnərsta:k]
Friday	**Freitag** (m)	['fraɪta:k]
Saturday	**Samstag** (m)	['zamsta:k]
Sunday	**Sonntag** (m)	['zɔnta:k]
today (adv)	**heute**	['hɔɪtə]
tomorrow (adv)	**morgen**	['mɔrgən]
the day after tomorrow	**übermorgen**	['ju:bər'mɔrgən]
yesterday (adv)	**gestern**	['gɛstərn]
the day before yesterday	**vorgestern**	['fo:rgəstərn]
day	**Tag** (m)	[ta:k]
working day	**Arbeitstag** (m)	['arbaɪtsta:k]
public holiday	**Feiertag** (m)	['fajərta:k]
day off	**freier Tag** (m)	['fraɪə ta:k]
weekend	**Wochenende** (n)	['vɔhə'nɛndə]
all day long	**den ganzen Tag**	[den 'gantsən 'ta:k]
next day (adv)	**am nächsten Tag**	[am 'nɛkstən ta:k]
two days ago	**zwei Tage vorher**	[tsvaɪ 'tagə 'fo:hə]
the day before	**am Vortag**	[am 'fɔrta:k]
daily (adj)	**täglich**	['tɛglifi]
every day (adv)	**täglich**	['tɛglifi]
week	**Woche** (f)	['vɔhə]
last week (adv)	**letzte Woche**	['lɛtstə 'vɔhə]
next week (adv)	**nächste Woche**	['nɛkstə 'vɔhə]
weekly (adj)	**wöchentlich**	['wøhəntlifi]
every week (adv)	**wöchentlich**	['wøhəntlifi]
twice a week	**zweimal pro Woche**	['tsvaɪma:l prɔ 'vɔhə]
every Tuesday	**jeden Dienstag**	['je:dən 'di:nsta:k]

20. Hours. Day and night

morning	**Morgen** (m)	['mɔrgən]
in the morning	**morgens**	['mɔrgəns]
noon, midday	**Mittag** (m)	['mita:k]

in the afternoon	nachmittags	['naːhmiˈtaːks]
evening	Abend (m)	['aːbənt]
in the evening	abends	['aːbənts]
night	Nacht (f)	[naht]
at night	nachts	[nahts]
midnight	Mitternacht (f)	['mitə naht]

second	Sekunde (f)	[zeˈkʊndə]
minute	Minute (f)	[miˈnuːtə]
hour	Stunde (f)	['ʃtʊndə]
half an hour	eine halbe Stunde	['aɪnə 'halbə 'ʃtʊndə]
quarter of an hour	Viertelstunde (f)	['fɪrtəlʃtʊndə]
fifteen minutes	fünfzehn Minuten	['fynftseːn miˈnuːtən]
24 hours	Tag und Nacht	['taːk ʊnt 'naht]

sunrise	Sonnenaufgang (m)	['zɔnən 'aufgaŋ]
dawn	Morgendämmerung (f)	['mɔrgən 'dɛmərʊŋ]
early morning	früher Morgen (m)	['fryːə 'mɔrgən]
sunset	Sonnenuntergang (m)	['zɔnən 'untergaŋ]

early in the morning	früh am Morgen	[fryː am 'mɔrgən]
this morning	heute morgen	['hɔɪtə 'mɔrgən]
tomorrow morning	morgen früh	['mɔrgən 'fryː]

this afternoon	heute Mittag	['hɔɪtə 'mitaːk]
in the afternoon	nachmittags	['naːhmiˈtaːks]
tomorrow afternoon	morgen Nachmittag	['mɔrgən 'nahmitaːg]

| tonight (this evening) | heute Abend | ['hɔɪtə 'aːbənt] |
| tomorrow night | morgen Abend | ['mɔrgən 'aːbənt] |

at 3 o'clock sharp	Punkt drei Uhr	[pʊŋkt 'draɪ uːr]
about 4 o'clock	gegen vier Uhr	['geːgn fiːə uːr]
by 12 o'clock	um zwölf Uhr	[um 'tswølf 'uːr]

in 20 minutes	in zwanzig Minuten	[in 'tsvantsiɦ miˈnuːtən]
in an hour	in einer Stunde	[in 'aɪnə 'ʃtʊndə]
on time (adv)	rechtzeitig	['rɛhtsaɪtiɦ]

a quarter of ...	Viertel vor ...	['fɪrtəl for]
within an hour	innerhalb einer Stunde	['inərhalp 'aɪnə 'ʃtʊndə]
every 15 minutes	alle fünfzehn Minuten	['ale 'fynftseːn miˈnuːtən]
round the clock	Tag und Nacht	['taːk ʊnt 'naht]

21. Months. Seasons

January	Januar (m)	['janʊaːr]
February	Februar (m)	['feːbrʊaːr]
March	März (m)	[mɛrts]
April	April (m)	[apˈril]

| May | **Mai** (m) | [maɪ] |
| June | **Juni** (m) | ['juːni] |

July	**Juli** (m)	['juːli]
August	**August** (m)	[aʊ'ɡʊst]
September	**September** (m)	[zɛp'tɛmbə]
October	**Oktober** (m)	[ɔk'toːbə]
November	**November** (m)	[nɔ'vɛmbə]
December	**Dezember** (m)	[de'ʦɛmbə]

spring	**Frühling** (m)	['fryːlɪŋ]
in spring	**im Frühling**	[im 'fryːlɪŋ]
spring (as adj)	**Frühlings-**	['fryːlɪŋs]

summer	**Sommer** (m)	['zɔmə]
in summer	**im Sommer**	[im 'zɔmə]
summer (as adj)	**Sommer-**	['zɔmər]

fall	**Herbst** (m)	[hɛrpst]
in fall	**im Herbst**	[im hɛrpst]
fall (as adj)	**Herbst-**	[hɛrpst]

winter	**Winter** (m)	['wintə]
in winter	**im Winter**	[im 'wintə]
winter (as adj)	**Winter-**	['wintə]

month	**Monat** (m)	['moːnat]
this month	**in diesem Monat**	[in 'dizəm 'moːnat]
next month	**nächsten Monat**	['nɛhstən 'moːnat]
last month	**letzten Monat**	['lɛtstən 'moːnat]

a month ago	**vor einem Monat**	[for 'aɪnəm 'moːnat]
in a month	**über eine Monat**	['juːbə 'aɪnə 'moːnat]
in two months	**über zwei Monaten**	['juːbə ʦvaɪ 'moːnatən]
the whole month	**einen ganzen Monat**	['aɪnən 'ɡantsən 'moːnat]
all month long	**einen ganzen Monat**	['aɪnən 'ɡantsən 'moːnat]

monthly (~ magazine)	**monatlich**	['moːnatliɦ]
monthly (adv)	**monatlich**	['moːnatliɦ]
every month	**jeden Monat**	['jeːdən 'moːnat]
twice a month	**zweimal pro Monat**	['ʦvaɪmaːl pro 'moːnat]

year	**Jahr** (n)	[jaːr]
this year	**dieses Jahr**	['dizəs jaːr]
next year	**nächstes Jahr**	['nɛhstəs jaːr]
last year	**voriges Jahr**	['forigəs jar]

a year ago	**vor einem Jahr**	[for 'aɪnəm jaːr]
in a year	**über ein Jahr**	['juːbə aɪn jar]
in two years	**über zwei Jahre**	['juːbə ʦvaɪ 'jarə]
the whole year	**ein ganzes Jahr**	[aɪn 'ɡantsəs jaːr]
all year long	**ein ganzes Jahr**	[aɪn 'ɡantsəs jaːr]

every year	jedes Jahr	['je:dəs ja:r]
annual (adj)	jährlich	['jɛrliɦ]
annually (adv)	jährlich	['jɛrliɦ]
4 times a year	viermal pro Jahr	['fir'mal prɔ ja:r]

date (e.g., today's ~)	Datum (n)	['da:tʊm]
date (e.g., ~ of birth)	Datum (n)	['da:tʊm]
calendar	Kalender (m)	[ka'lendə]

half a year	ein halbes Jahr	[aɪn 'halbəs ja:r]
six months	Halbjahr (n)	[halp 'ja:r]
season (summer, etc.)	Saison (f)	[ɛɛ'zɔ.ɦ]
century	Jahrhundert (n)	[ja:r 'hʊndərt]

22. Units of measurement

weight	Gewicht (n)	['gəwiɦt]
length	Länge (f)	['lɛŋə]
width	Breite (f)	['braɪtə]
height	Höhe (f)	['hø:ə]
depth	Tiefe (f)	['ti:fə]
volume	Volumen (n)	[vɔ'ly:mən]
area	Fläche (f)	['flɛhə]

gram	Gramm (n)	[gram]
milligram	Milligramm (n)	[milig'ram]
kilogram	Kilo (n)	['kilɔ]
ton	Tonne (f)	['tɔnə]
pound	Pfund (n)	[pfʊnt]
ounce	Unze (f)	['untsə]

meter	Meter (m)	['me:tə]
millimeter	Millimeter (m)	[mili'me:tə]
centimeter	Zentimeter (m)	[tsɛnti'me:tə]
kilometer	Kilometer (m)	[kilɔ'me:tə]
mile	Meile (f)	['maɪlə]

inch	Zoll (m)	[tsɔl]
foot	Fuß (m)	[fʊ:s]
yard	Yard (n)	[jart]

| square meter | Quadratmeter (m) | [kvad'rat 'metə] |
| hectare | Hektar (n) | [hɛk'ta:r] |

liter	Liter (m)	['li:tə]
degree	Grad (m)	[grat]
volt	Volt (n)	[vɔlt]
ampere	Ampere (n)	[am'pɛ:r]
horsepower	Pferdestärke (f)	['pfe:rdə 'ʃtɛrkə]
quantity	Anzahl (f)	['antsal]

a little bit of ...	etwas ...	['ɛtvas]
half	Hälfte (f)	['hɛlftə]
dozen	Dutzend (n)	['dʊtsənt]
piece (item)	Stück (n)	[ʃtyk]
size	Größe (f)	['grøsə]
scale (map ~)	Maßstab (m)	['ma:sʃta:p]
minimal (adj)	minimal	[mini'ma:l]
the smallest (adj)	der kleinste	[də 'klaɪnstə]
medium (adj)	mittler, mittel-	['mitlə], ['mitl]
maximal (adj)	maximal	[maksi'ma:l]
the largest (adj)	der größte	[də 'grø:stə]

23. Containers

jar (glass)	Glas (n)	[gla:s]
can	Dose (f)	['do:zə]
bucket	Eimer (m)	['aɪmə]
barrel	Fass (n), Tonne (f)	[fas], ['tɔnə]
basin (for washing)	Waschschüssel (n)	[vaʃ 'ʃy:sl]
tank (for liquid, gas)	Behälter (m)	['bəhɛltə]
hip flask	Flachmann (m)	['flahman]
jerrycan	Kanister (m)	[ka'nistə]
cistern (tank)	Zisterne (f)	[tsis'tɛrnə]
mug	Kaffeebecher (m)	['kafe bəhə]
cup (of coffee, etc.)	Tasse (f)	['tasə]
saucer	Untertasse (f)	['untər'tasə]
glass (tumbler)	Wasserglas (n)	['vasəg'ʎa:s]
wineglass	Weinglas (n)	['vaɪn la:s]
saucepan	Kochtopf (m)	['kɔhtɔpf]
bottle (~ of wine)	Flasche (f)	['fla:ʃə]
neck (of the bottle)	Flaschenhals (m)	['fla:ʃənhals]
carafe	Karaffe (f)	[ka'rafə]
pitcher (earthenware)	Tonkrug (m)	[tɔŋk'rʊk]
vessel (container)	Gefäß (n)	['gəfɛs]
pot (crock)	Topf (m)	[tɔpf]
vase	Vase (f)	['va:zə]
bottle (~ of perfume)	Flakon (n)	[fla'kɔn]
vial, small bottle	Fläschchen (n)	['flɛʃhən]
tube (of toothpaste)	Tube (f)	['tu:bə]
sack (bag)	Sack (m)	[zak]
bag (paper ~, plastic ~)	Tüte (f)	['ty:tə]
box (e.g., shoebox)	Karton (m)	[kar'tɔn]

| crate | **Kiste** (f) | ['kistə] |
| basket | **Korb** (m) | [kɔrp] |

HUMAN BEING

Human being. The body

24. Head

head	**Kopf** (m)	[kɔpf]
face	**Gesicht** (n)	['ɡəziħt]
nose	**Nase** (f)	['na:zə]
mouth	**Mund** (m)	[mʊnt]
eye	**Auge** (n)	['augə]
eyes	**Augen** (pl)	['augən]
pupil	**Pupille** (f)	[pʊ'pilə]
eyebrow	**Augenbraue** (f)	['augənbrauə]
eyelash	**Wimper** (f)	['wimpə]
eyelid	**Augenlid** (n)	['augənlit]
tongue	**Zunge** (f)	['tsuŋə]
tooth	**Zahn** (m)	[tsa:n]
lips	**Lippen** (pl)	['lipən]
cheekbones	**Backenknochen** (pl)	['bakəŋknɔhn]
gum	**Zahnfleisch** (n)	['tsa:nflaıʃ]
palate	**Gaumen** (m)	['gaumən]
nostrils	**Nasenlöcher** (pl)	['na:zənløhə]
chin	**Kinn** (n)	[kin]
jaw	**Kiefer** (m)	['ki:fə]
cheek	**Wange** (f)	['vaŋə]
forehead	**Stirn** (f)	[ʃtirn]
temple	**Schläfe** (f)	['ʃlɛfə]
ear	**Ohr** (n)	[ɔ:r]
back of the head	**Nacken** (m)	['nakən]
neck	**Hals** (m)	[hals]
throat	**Kehle** (f)	['ke:lə]
hair	**Haare** (pl)	['ha:arə]
hairstyle	**Frisur** (f)	[fri'zu:r]
haircut	**Haarschnitt** (m)	['ha:rʃnit]
wig	**Perücke** (f)	[pe'rykə]
mustache	**Schnurrbart** (m)	['ʃnʊrba:rt]
beard	**Bart** (m)	[bart]
to have (a beard, etc.)	**haben** (vt)	[ha:bn]

| braid | Zopf (m) | [tsɔpf] |
| sideburns | Backenbart (m) | ['bakənbaːrt] |

red-haired (adj)	rothaarig	['roːthaːriɦ]
gray (hair)	grau	['grau]
bald (adj)	kahl	[kaːl]
bald patch	Glatze (f)	['glatsə]

| ponytail | Pferdeschwanz (m) | ['pfeːrdə ʃvants] |
| bangs | Pony (m) | ['pɔni] |

25. Human body

| hand | Hand (f) | [hant] |
| arm | Arm (m) | [arm] |

finger	Finger (m)	['fiŋə]
thumb	Daumen (m)	['daumən]
little finger	kleiner Finger (m)	['klaɪnə 'fiŋə]
nail	Nagel (m)	['naːgəl]

fist	Faust (f)	['faust]
palm	Handfläche (f)	['hantf'lɛhə]
wrist	Handgelenk (n)	['hantgələŋk]
forearm	Unterarm (m)	['untərarm]
elbow	Ellbogen (m)	['ɛlboːgən]
shoulder	Schulter (f)	['ʃʊltə]

leg	Bein (n)	[baɪn]
foot	Fuß (m)	[fʊːs]
knee	Knie (n)	[kniː]
calf (part of leg)	Wade (f)	['vaːdə]
hip	Hüfte (f)	['hyftə]
heel	Ferse (f)	['fɛrzə]

body	Körper (m)	['kørpə]
stomach	Bauch (m)	['bauh]
chest	Brust (f)	[brʊst]
breast	Busen (m)	['buːzən]
flank	Seite (f), Flanke (f)	['zaɪtə], ['flaŋkə]
back	Rücken (m)	['rykən]
lower back	Kreuz (n)	['krɔɪts]
waist	Taille (f)	['taʎə]

navel	Nabel (m)	['naːbl]
buttocks	Gesäße (pl)	['gəzɛːs]
bottom	Hinterteil (n)	['hintə taɪl]

| beauty mark | Leberfleck (m) | ['leːbəflək] |
| birthmark | Muttermal (n) | ['mʊtərmaːl] |

tattoo	**Tätowierung** (f)	[tɛto'wiːrʊŋ]
scar	**Narbe** (f)	['narbə]

Clothing & Accessories

26. Outerwear. Coats

clothes	**Kleidung** (f)	['klaɪdʊŋ]
outer clothes	**Oberkleidung** (f)	['ɔːbɐ 'klaɪdʊŋ]
winter clothes	**Winterkleidung** (f)	['wintɐ 'klaɪdʊŋ]
overcoat	**Mantel** (m)	['mantl]
fur coat	**Pelzmantel** (m)	['pɛlts mantl]
fur jacket	**Pelzjacke** (f)	[pɛlts 'jakə]
down coat	**Daunenjacke** (f)	['daunən 'jakə]
jacket (e.g., leather ~)	**Jacke** (f)	['jakə]
raincoat	**Regenmantel** (m)	['reːgən 'mantl]
waterproof (adj)	**wasserdicht**	['vasə'diht]

27. Men's & women's clothing

shirt	**Hemd** (n)	[hɛmt]
pants	**Hose** (f)	['hɔːzə]
jeans	**Jeans** (pl)	[dʒins]
jacket (of man's suit)	**Jackett** (n)	[ja'ket]
suit	**Anzug** (m)	['antsuːk]
dress (frock)	**Kleid** (n)	[klaɪt]
skirt	**Rock** (m)	[rɔk]
blouse	**Bluse** (f)	['bluːzə]
knitted jacket	**Strickjacke** (f)	['ʃtrik 'jakə]
jacket (of woman's suit)	**Jacke** (f)	['jakə]
T-shirt	**T-Shirt** (n)	['tiːʃɔːt]
shorts (short trousers)	**Shorts** (pl)	[ʃɔrts]
tracksuit	**Sportanzug** (m)	['ʃport 'antsuːk]
bathrobe	**Bademantel** (m)	['baːdə mantl]
pajamas	**Schlafanzug** (m)	[ʃlaf 'antsuːk]
sweater	**Sweater** (m)	['svɛtə]
pullover	**Pullover** (m)	[pʊ'lɔːvə]
vest	**Weste** (f)	['vɛstə]
tailcoat	**Frack** (m)	[frak]
tuxedo	**Smoking** (m)	['smɔːkiŋ]
uniform	**Uniform** (f)	['uniform]

workwear	**Arbeitskleidung** (f)	['arbaɪts klaɪdʊŋ]
overalls	**Overall** (m)	['ɔːvərɔːl]
coat (e.g., doctor's smock)	**Kittel** (m)	['kitl]

28. Clothing. Underwear

underwear	**Unterwäsche** (f)	['untərvɛʃə]
undershirt (A-shirt)	**Unterhemd** (n)	['untəhəmt]
socks	**Socken** (pl)	['zɔkən]

nightgown	**Nachthemd** (n)	['nahthɛmt]
bra	**Büstenhalter** (m)	['bystən'haltə]
knee highs	**Kniestrümpfe** (pl)	['kniːʃtrympfə]
tights	**Strumpfhose** (f)	['ʃtrʊmpfhɔːzə]
stockings (thigh highs)	**Strümpfe** (pl)	['ʃtrympfə]
bathing suit	**Badeanzug** (m)	['baːdə 'antsuːk]

29. Headwear

hat	**Mütze** (f)	['mytsə]
fedora	**Filzhut** (m)	['filtshʊt]
baseball cap	**Baseballkappe** (f)	['bɛɪzbɔl 'kapə]
flatcap	**Schiebermütze** (f)	['ʃiːbə'mytsə]

beret	**Baskenmütze** (f)	['baskən'mytsə]
hood	**Kapuze** (f)	[ka'puːtsə]
panama hat	**Panamahut** (m)	['panama 'hʊt]
knitted hat	**Strickmütze** (f)	['ʃtrikmytsə]

| headscarf | **Kopftuch** (n) | ['kɔpftʊːh] |
| women's hat | **Damenhut** (m) | ['daːmən'hʊːt] |

hard hat	**Schutzhelm** (m)	['ʃʊtshɛlm]
garrison cap	**Feldmütze** (f)	['fɛlt'mytsə]
helmet	**Helm** (m)	[hɛlm]

| derby | **Melone** (f) | [me'lɔːnə] |
| top hat | **Zylinder** (m) | [tsy'lində] |

30. Footwear

footwear	**Schuhe** (pl)	['ʃʊːə]
ankle boots	**Stiefeletten** (pl)	[ʃtif'letən]
shoes (low-heeled ~)	**Halbschuhe** (pl)	['halpʃʊːə]
boots (cowboy ~)	**Stiefel** (pl)	['ʃtiːfl]
slippers	**Hausschuhe** (pl)	['haus ʃʊːə]

tennis shoes	Tennisschuhe (pl)	['tɛnis'ʃuːə]
sneakers	Leinenschuhe (pl)	['laɪnən 'ʃuːə]
sandals	Sandalen (pl)	[zan'dalən]

cobbler	Schuster (m)	['ʃustə]
heel	Absatz (m)	['apzats]
pair (of shoes)	Paar (n)	['paːr]

shoestring	Schnürsenkel (m)	['ʃnyːrzɛŋkl]
to lace (vt)	schnüren (vt)	['ʃnyːrən]
shoehorn	Schuhlöffel (m)	['ʃuːløfl]
shoe polish	Schuhcreme (f)	['ʃuːkreːm]

31. Personal accessories

gloves	Handschuhe (pl)	['hantʃuːə]
mittens	Fausthandschuhe (pl)	['faust'hantʃuːə]
scarf (muffler)	Schal (m)	[ʃaːl]

glasses	Brille (f)	['brilə]
frame (eyeglass ~)	Brillengestell (n)	['brilen`eʃtəl]
umbrella	Regenschirm (m)	['reːgən'ʃirm]
walking stick	Spazierstock (m)	[ʃpaˈtsiːrʃtɔk]
hairbrush	Haarbürste (f)	['haːr'byrstə]
fan	Fächer (m)	['fɛhə]

necktie	Krawatte (f)	[kra'vatə]
bow tie	Fliege (f)	['fliːgə]
suspenders	Hosenträger (pl)	['hɔːzəntrɛgə]
handkerchief	Taschentuch (n)	['taʃən'tuh]

comb	Kamm (m)	[kam]
barrette	Haarspange (f)	['haːrʃpaŋə]
hairpin	Haarnadel (f)	['haːrnaːdl]
buckle	Schnalle (f)	['ʃnalə]

| belt | Gürtel (m) | ['gyrtl] |
| shoulder strap | Umhängegurt (m) | [um'hɛŋəgurt] |

bag (handbag)	Tasche (f)	['taʃə]
purse	Handtasche (f)	['han'taʃə]
backpack	Rucksack (m)	['rukzak]

32. Clothing. Miscellaneous

fashion	Mode (f)	['mɔːdə]
in vogue (adj)	modisch	['mɔːdiʃ]
fashion designer	Modedesigner (m)	['mɔːdə di'zaɪnə]

collar	Kragen (m)	['kra:gən]
pocket	Tasche (f)	['taʃə]
pocket (as adj)	Taschen-	['taʃən]
sleeve	Ärmel (m)	['ɛrml]
hanging loop	Aufhänger (m)	['aufhəŋə]
fly (on trousers)	Hosenschlitz (m)	['ho:zənʃlits]
zipper (fastener)	Reißverschluss (m)	['raisfɛrʃ'lys]
fastener	Verschluss (m)	[fɛrʃ'lys]
button	Knopf (m)	[knɔpf]
buttonhole	Knopfloch (n)	['knɔpflɔh]
to come off (ab. button)	abgehen (vi)	['apge:ən]
to sew (vi, vt)	nähen (vi, vt)	['nɛ:ən]
to embroider (vi, vt)	sticken (vt)	['ʃtikən]
embroidery	Stickerei (f)	[ʃtikə'rai]
sewing needle	Nadel (f)	['na:dəl]
thread	Faden (m)	['fa:dən]
seam	Naht (f)	[na:t]
to get dirty (vi)	sich beschmutzen	[ziɦ 'bəʃmʊtsən]
stain (mark, spot)	Fleck (m)	[flɛk]
to crease, crumple (vi)	sich knittern	[ziɦ 'knitərn]
to tear (vt)	zerreißen (vt)	[tsɛ'raisən]
clothes moth	Motte (f)	['mɔtə]

33. Personal care. Cosmetics

toothpaste	Zahnpasta (f)	['tsa:n'pasta]
toothbrush	Zahnbürste (f)	['tsa:nbyrstə]
to brush one's teeth	Zähne putzen	['tsɛ:nə 'pʊtsən]
razor	Rasierer (m)	[ra'zi:rə]
shaving cream	Rasiercreme (f)	[ra'zi:rkrɛ:m]
to shave (vi)	sich rasieren	[ziɦ ra'zi:rən]
soap	Seife (f)	['zaifə]
shampoo	Shampoo (n)	[ʃam'po:]
scissors	Schere (f)	['ʃɛrə]
nail file	Nagelfeile (f)	['na:gəl failə]
nail clippers	Nagelzange (f)	['na:gəl tsaŋə]
tweezers	Pinzette (f)	[pin'tsɛtə]
cosmetics	Kosmetik (f)	[kɔs'me:tik]
face mask	Gesichtsmaske (f)	['gəziɦts 'ma:skə]
manicure	Maniküre (f)	[mani'ky:rə]
to have a manicure	Maniküre machen	[mani'ky:rə 'mahn]
pedicure	Pediküre (f)	[pedi'ky:rə]
make-up bag	Kosmetiktasche (f)	[kɔs'me:tik 'taʃə]

face powder	**Puder** (m)	['pʊːdə]
powder compact	**Puderdose** (f)	['pʊːdə'dɔːzə]
blusher	**Rouge** (n)	[rʊːʒ]

perfume (bottled)	**Parfüm** (n)	[par'fyːm]
toilet water (perfume)	**Duftwasser** (n)	['dʊftvasə]
lotion	**Lotion** (f)	[lɔ'tsɔːn]
cologne	**Kölnischwasser** (n)	['kølniʃ 'vasə]

eyeshadow	**Lidschatten** (m)	['lit'ʃatən]
eyeliner	**Kajalstift** (m)	['kajalʃtift]
mascara	**Wimperntusche** (f)	['wimpɛrn'tuʃə]

lipstick	**Lippenstift** (m)	['lipənʃtift]
nail polish, enamel	**Nagellack** (m)	['naːgəl lak]
hair spray	**Haarlack** (m)	['haːrlak]
deodorant	**Deodorant** (n)	[deodo'rant]

cream	**Creme** (f)	[krɛːm]
face cream	**Gesichtscreme** (f)	['gəziħts krɛːm]
hand cream	**Handcreme** (f)	['hantkrɛːm]
anti-wrinkle cream	**Anti-Falten-Creme** (f)	['anti 'faltən krɛːm]
day (as adj)	**Tages-**	['taːgəs]
night (as adj)	**Nacht-**	[naht]

tampon	**Tampon** (m)	[tam'pɔn]
toilet paper	**Toilettenpapier** (n)	[tɔa'letən pa'piːə]
hair dryer	**Fön** (m)	['føːn]

34. Watches. Clocks

watch (wristwatch)	**Armbanduhr** (f)	['armbant 'uːr]
dial	**Zifferblatt** (n)	['tsifərb'lat]
hand (of clock, watch)	**Zeiger** (m)	['tsaigə]
metal watch band	**Metallarmband** (n)	[me'tal 'aːmbant]
watch strap	**Uhrenarmband** (n)	['uːrən aːmbant]

battery	**Batterie** (f)	[batə'riː]
to change a battery	**die Batterie wechseln**	[di batə'riː 'vɛksəln]
to run fast	**vorgehen** (vi)	['foːrgeːən]
to run slow	**nachgehen** (vi)	['nahgeːən]

wall clock	**Wanduhr** (f)	['vant uːr]
hourglass	**Sanduhr** (f)	['zant uːr]
sundial	**Sonnenuhr** (f)	['zɔnən uːr]
alarm clock	**Wecker** (m)	['vɛkə]
watchmaker	**Uhrmacher** (m)	['uːrmahə]
to repair (vt)	**reparieren** (vt)	[repa'riːrən]

Food. Nutricion

35. Food

meat	Fleisch (n)	[flaɪʃ]
chicken	Hühnerfleisch (n)	['hyːnərflaɪʃ]
young chicken	Küken (n)	['kyːkən]
duck	Ente (f)	['ɛntə]
goose	Gans (f)	[gans]
game	Wild (n)	[wilt]
turkey	Pute (f)	['puːtə]
pork	Schweinefleisch (n)	['ʃvaɪnəflaɪʃ]
veal	Kalbfleisch (n)	['kalpfˈlaɪʃ]
lamb	Hammelfleisch (n)	['haməlflaɪʃ]
beef	Rindfleisch (n)	['rintfˈlaɪʃ]
rabbit	Kaninchen (n)	[ka'ninhən]
sausage (salami, etc.)	Wurst (f)	[vʊrst]
vienna sausage	Würstchen (n)	['wyrsthən]
bacon	Schinkenspeck (m)	['ʃiŋkən ʃpək]
ham	Schinken (m)	['ʃiŋkən]
gammon (ham)	Räucherschinken (m)	['rɔɪheˈʃiŋkən]
pâté	Pastete (f)	[pas'teːtə]
liver	Leber (f)	['leːbə]
lard	Speck (m)	[ʃpɛk]
ground beef	Hackfleisch (n)	['hakfˈlaɪʃ]
tongue	Zunge (f)	['tsʊŋə]
egg	Ei (n)	[aɪ]
eggs	Eier (pl)	['aɪə]
egg white	Eiweiß (n)	['aɪˈvaɪs]
egg yolk	Eigelb (n)	['aɪˈgɛlp]
fish	Fisch (m)	[fiʃ]
seafood	Meeresfrüchte (pl)	['meːərəsfˈryhtə]
crustaceans	Krebstiere (pl)	['kreːpstiːrə]
caviar	Kaviar (m)	['kaːwiaːr]
crab	Krabbe (f)	['krabə]
shrimp	Garnele (f)	[gar'nɛlə]
oyster	Auster (f)	['austə]
spiny lobster	Languste (f)	[laŋ 'ʊstə]
octopus	Krake (m)	['kraːkə]

squid	Kalmar (m)	['kalmar]
sturgeon	Störfleisch (n)	[ʃtørf'laiʃ]
salmon	Lachs (m)	[laks]
halibut	Heilbutt (m)	['hail'bʊt]

cod	Dorsch (m)	[dɔrʃ]
mackerel	Makrele (f)	[mak'rɛlə]
tuna	Tunfisch (m)	['tʊn'fiʃ]
eel	Aal (m)	[a:l]

| trout | Forelle (f) | [fo'rɛ:lə] |
| sardine | Sardine (f) | [zar'dinə] |

| pike | Hecht (m) | [hɛht] |
| herring | Hering (m) | ['he:riŋ] |

| bread | Brot (n) | [brɔ:t] |
| cheese | Käse (m) | ['kɛzə] |

| sugar | Zucker (m) | ['tsukə] |
| salt | Salz (n) | [zalts] |

rice	Reis (m)	[rais]
pasta	Teigwaren (pl)	[taih'varən]
noodles	Nudeln (pl)	['nʊ:dəln]

butter	Butter (f)	['bʊtə]
vegetable oil	Pflanzenöl (n)	[pflantsn ø:l]
sunflower oil	Sonnenblumenöl (n)	['zɔnən 'blymən øl]
margarine	Margarine (f)	[marga'ri:nə]

| olives | Oliven (pl) | [ɔ'li:vən] |
| olive oil | Olivenöl (n) | [ɔ'li:vən ø:l] |

milk	Milch (f)	[milh]
condensed milk	Kondensmilch (f)	[kɔn'dɛns'milh]
yogurt	Joghurt (m)	['jogʊrt]

| sour cream | saure Sahne (f) | ['zaurə 'zanə] |
| cream (of milk) | Sahne (f) | ['za:nə] |

| mayonnaise | Mayonnaise (f) | [majɔ'nɛ:zə] |
| buttercream | Buttercreme (f) | ['bʊtəkrɛ:m] |

cereal grain (wheat, etc.)	Grütze (f)	['grytsə]
flour	Mehl (n)	[me:l]
canned food	Konserven (pl)	[kɔn'zɛrvən]

cornflakes	Haferflocken (pl)	['ha:fərf'lɔkən]
honey	Honig (m)	['hɔ:nih]
jam	Marmelade (f)	[marmə'la:də]
chewing gum	Kaugummi (m, n)	['kaugʊmi]

36. Drinks

water	Wasser (n)	['vasə]
drinking water	Trinkwasser (n)	['triŋk 'vasə]
mineral water	Mineralwasser (n)	[mine'ra:l 'vasə]

still (adj)	still	[ʃtil]
carbonated (adj)	mit Kohlensäure	[mit 'kɔlen'zɔjerə]
sparkling (adj)	mit Gas	[mit 'ga:s]
ice	Eis (n)	[aɪs]
with ice	mit Eis	[mit aɪs]

non-alcoholic (adj)	alkoholfrei	['alkɔhɔ:l 'fraɪ]
soft drink	alkoholfreies Getränk (n)	['alkɔhɔ:l 'fraɪes 'gətrɛŋk]
cool soft drink	Erfrischungsgetränk (n)	[ɛrf'riʃʊŋs get'rɛŋk]
lemonade	Limonade (f)	[limɔ'na:də]

liquor	Spirituosen (pl)	[ʃpiritʊ'ɔ:zən]
wine	Wein (m)	[vaɪn]
white wine	Weißwein (m)	['vaɪsvaɪn]
red wine	Rotwein (m)	['rɔ:t'vaɪn]

liqueur	Likör (m)	[li'kø:r]
champagne	Champagner (m)	[ʃam'paɲə]
vermouth	Wermut (m)	['we:rmʊ:t]

whisky	Whisky (m)	['wiski]
vodka	Wodka (m)	['vɔtka]
gin	Gin (m)	[dʒin]
cognac	Kognak (m)	['kɔɲjak]
rum	Rum (m)	[rʊm]

coffee	Kaffee (m)	['kafe]
black coffee	schwarzer Kaffee (m)	['ʃvartsə 'kafe]
coffee with milk	Milchkaffee (m)	['milħ 'kafe]
cappuccino	Cappuccino (m)	[kapʊ'tʃi:nɔ]
instant coffee	Pulverkaffee (m)	['pʊlvə 'kafe]

milk	Milch (f)	[milħ]
cocktail	Cocktail (m)	['kɔktəl]
milk shake	Milchcocktail (m)	['milħ 'kɔktəl]

juice	Saft (m)	[zaft]
tomato juice	Tomatensaft (m)	[tɔ'ma:tən zaft]
orange juice	Orangensaft (m)	[ɔ'ranʒənzaft]
freshly squeezed juice	frisch gepresster Saft (m)	[friʃ 'gəprɛstə zaft]

beer	Bier (n)	[bi:ə]
light beer	Helles (n)	['hɛles]
dark beer	Dunkelbier (n)	['dʊŋkl bi:ə]
tea	Tee (m)	[te:]

47

| black tea | schwarzer Tee (m) | ['ʃvartsə 'te:] |
| green tea | grüner Tee (m) | ['gry:nə te:] |

37. Vegetables

| vegetables | Gemüse (n) | ['gəmy:zə] |
| greens | grünes Gemüse (pl) | ['grynəs 'gəmy:zə] |

tomato	Tomate (f)	[to'ma:tə]
cucumber	Gurke (f)	['gʊrkə]
carrot	Karotte (f)	[ka'rɔtə]
potato	Kartoffel (f)	[kar'tɔ:fl]
onion	Zwiebel (f)	['tswi:bl]
garlic	Knoblauch (m)	['knɔblauh]

cabbage	Kohl (m)	[kɔ:l]
cauliflower	Blumenkohl (m)	['blu:mənkɔ:l]
Brussels sprouts	Rosenkohl (m)	['rɔ:zənkɔ:l]
broccoli	Brokkoli (pl)	['brɔkɔli]

beetroot	Zuckerrübe (f)	['tsukərry:bə]
eggplant	Aubergine (f)	[ɔbɛr'ʒi:nə]
zucchini	Zucchini (f)	[tsu'kini]
pumpkin	Kürbis (m)	['kyrbis]
turnip	Rübe (f)	['ry:bə]

parsley	Petersilie (f)	[petə'zi:liə]
dill	Dill (m)	[dil]
lettuce	Kopf Salat (m)	[kɔpf za'la:t]
celery	Sellerie (m)	['zɛləri]
asparagus	Spargel (m)	['ʃpargl]
spinach	Spinat (m)	[ʃpi'na:t]

pea	Erbse (f)	['ɛrpsə]
beans	Bohnen (pl)	['bɔ:nən]
corn (maize)	Mais (m)	['mais]
kidney bean	Weiße Bohne (f)	['vaisə 'bɔ:nə]

pepper	Spanischer Pfeffer (m)	['ʃpa:niʃə 'pfɛfə]
radish	Radieschen (n)	[ra'dishən]
artichoke	Artischocke (f)	[arti'ʃɔkə]

38. Fruits. Nuts

fruit	Frucht (f)	[frʊht]
apple	Apfel (m)	['apfl]
pear	Birne (f)	['birnə]
lemon	Zitrone (f)	[tsit'rɔ:nə]

| orange | **Apfelsine** (f) | [apfel'zi:nə] |
| strawberry | **Erdbeere** (f) | ['e:rt'be:rə] |

mandarin	**Mandarine** (f)	[manda'ri:nə]
plum	**Pflaume** (f)	['pflaumə]
peach	**Pfirsich** (m)	['pfɪrzɪħ]
apricot	**Aprikose** (f)	[apri'kɔ:zə]
raspberry	**Himbeere** (f)	['himbe:rə]
pineapple	**Ananas** (f)	['ananas]

banana	**Banane** (f)	[ba'na:nə]
watermelon	**Wassermelone** (f)	['vasəmə'lo:nə]
grape	**Weintrauben** (pl)	['vaɪntraubn]
sour cherry	**Sauerkirsche** (f)	['zauə'kɪrʃə]
sweet cherry	**Herzkirsche** (f)	[hɛrts'kɪrʃə]
melon	**Melone** (f)	[me'lo:nə]

grapefruit	**Grapefruit** (f)	['grɛɪpfrʊ:t]
avocado	**Avocado** (f)	[avo'ka:do]
papaya	**Papaya** (f)	[pa'paja]
mango	**Mango** (f)	['maŋ ɔ]
pomegranate	**Granatapfel** (m)	[grana:'tapfl]

redcurrant	**rote Johannisbeere** (f)	['rɔ:tə jɔ'hanis'be:rə]
blackcurrant	**schwarze**	['ʃvartsə
	Johannisbeere (f)	johanisbe:rə]
gooseberry	**Stachelbeere** (f)	['ʃtahelbe:rə]
bilberry	**Heidelbeere** (f)	['haɪdlbe:rə]
blackberry	**Brombeere** (f)	['brɔmbe:rə]

raisin	**Rosinen** (pl)	[rɔ'zi:nən]
fig	**Feige** (f)	['faɪgə]
date	**Dattel** (f)	['datl]

peanut	**Erdnuss** (f)	['e:rtnʊs]
almond	**Mandel** (f)	['mandl]
walnut	**Walnuss** (f)	['valnʊs]
hazelnut	**Haselnuss** (f)	['ha:zəlnʊs]
coconut	**Kokosnuss** (f)	['kɔkɔsnʊs]
pistachios	**Pistazien** (pl)	[pis'tatsien]

39. Bread. Candy

confectionery (pastry)	**Konditorwaren** (pl)	[kɔnditɔr'va:rən]
bread	**Brot** (n)	[brɔ:t]
cookies	**Keks** (m)	[ke:ks]

chocolate (n)	**Schokolade** (f)	[ʃɔkɔ'la:də]
chocolate (as adj)	**Schokoladen-**	[ʃɔkɔ'la:dən]
candy	**Bonbon** (m, n)	[bɔn'bɔn]

cake (e.g., cupcake)	**Törtchen** (n)	['tørthən]
cake (e.g., birthday ~)	**Torte** (f)	['tɔrtə]
pie (e.g., apple ~)	**Kuchen** (m)	['kuːhən]
filling (for cake, pie)	**Füllung** (f)	['fyːluŋ]
whole fruit jam	**Konfitüre** (f)	[kɔnfi'tyːrə]
marmalade	**Marmelade** (f)	[marmə'laːdə]
waffle	**Waffeln** (pl)	['vafəln]
ice-cream	**Eis** (n)	[aɪs]
pudding	**Pudding** (m)	['puːdiŋ]

40. Cooked dishes

course, dish	**Gericht** (n)	['gəriht]
cuisine	**Küche** (f)	['kyhə]
recipe	**Rezept** (n)	[re'tsɛpt]
portion	**Portion** (f)	[pɔr'tsjoːn]
salad	**Salat** (m)	[za'laːt]
soup	**Suppe** (f)	['zupə]
clear soup (broth)	**Brühe** (f), **Bouillon** (f)	['bryə], [buˈʎɔn]
sandwich (bread)	**belegtes Brot** (n)	['bəleːktəs brot]
fried eggs	**Spiegelei** (n)	['ʃpiːgəlaɪ]
cutlet (croquette)	**Kotelett** (n)	[kotə'let]
hamburger (beefburger)	**Hamburger** (m)	['hamburgə]
beefsteak	**Beefsteak** (n)	['biːfstɛɪk]
stew	**Braten** (m)	['braːtən]
side dish	**Beilage** (f)	['baɪlaːgə]
spaghetti	**Spaghetti** (pl)	[spa'geti]
mashed potatoes	**Kartoffelpüree** (n)	[kar'tɔːfəl pyreː]
pizza	**Pizza** (f)	['pitsa]
porridge (oatmeal, etc.)	**Brei** (m)	[braɪ]
omelet	**Omelett** (n)	[ɔm'lɛt]
boiled (e.g., ~ beef)	**gekocht**	['gəkoht]
smoked (adj)	**geräuchert**	['gərɔɪhert]
fried (adj)	**gebraten**	['gəbraːtən]
dried (adj)	**getrocknet**	['gətrɔknət]
frozen (adj)	**tiefgekühlt**	['tiːfgə'kyːlt]
pickled (adj)	**mariniert**	[mari'niːrt]
sweet (sugary)	**süß**	[zyːs]
salty (adj)	**salzig**	['zaltsih]
cold (adj)	**kalt**	[kalt]
hot (adj)	**heiß**	[haɪs]
bitter (adj)	**bitter**	['bitə]

tasty (adj)	lecker	['lɛkə]
to cook in boiling water	kochen (vt)	['kɔhn]
to cook (dinner)	zubereiten (vt)	['ʦuːbəraɪtən]
to fry (vt)	braten (vt)	['braːtən]
to heat up (food)	aufwärmen (vt)	['aʊfvɛrmən]

to salt (vt)	salzen (vt)	['zaltsən]
to pepper (vt)	pfeffern (vt)	['pfɛfərn]
to grate (vt)	reiben (vt)	[raɪbn]
peel (n)	Schale (f)	['ʃaːlə]
to peel (vt)	schälen (vt)	['ʃɛlən]

41. Spices

salt	Salz (n)	[zalts]
salty (adj)	salzig	['zaltsiḣ]
to salt (vt)	salzen (vt)	['zaltsən]

black pepper	schwarzer Pfeffer (m)	['ʃvartsə 'pfɛfə]
red pepper	Paprika (m)	['paprika]
mustard	Senf (m)	[zɛnf]
horseradish	Meerrettich (m)	['meːəˈrɛtiḣ]

condiment	Gewürz (n)	['gəwyrts]
spice	Würze (f)	['wyːrtsə]
sauce	Soße (f)	['zɔːsə]
vinegar	Essig (m)	['ɛsiḣ]

anise	Anis (m)	[aˈniːs]
basil	Basilikum (n)	[baˈziːlikʊm]
cloves	Nelke (f)	['nɛlkə]
ginger	Ingwer (m)	['iŋvə]
coriander	Koriander (m)	[kɔriˈandə]
cinnamon	Zimt (m)	[ʦimt]

sesame	Sesam (m)	['zeːzam]
bay leaf	Lorbeerblatt (n)	['lɔrbeːrblat]
paprika	Paprika (m)	['paprika]
caraway	Kümmel (m)	['kyml]
saffron	Safran (m)	['zafran]

42. Meals

| food | Essen (n) | ['ɛsn] |
| to eat (vi, vt) | essen (vi, vt) | ['ɛsn] |

| breakfast | Frühstück (n) | ['fryːʃtyk] |
| to have breakfast | frühstücken (vi) | ['fryːʃtykən] |

lunch	Mittagessen (n)	['mita:k 'ɛsən]
to have lunch	zu Mittag essen	[ʦu 'mita:k 'ɛsn]
dinner	Abendessen (n)	['a:bnt 'ɛsən]
to have dinner	zu Abend essen	[ʦu 'a:bənt 'ɛsn]

| appetite | Appetit (m) | [apə'ti:t] |
| Enjoy your meal! | Guten Appetit! | ['gu:tn apə'ti:t] |

to open (~ a bottle)	öffnen (vt)	[øfnən]
to spill (liquid)	verschütten (vt)	[fɛr'ʃy:tən]
to spill out (vi)	verschüttet werden	[fɛr'ʃy:tət 'we:rdən]

to boil (vi)	kochen (vi)	['kɔhn]
to boil (vt)	kochen (vt)	['kɔhn]
boiled (~ water)	gekocht	['gəkɔht]

| to chill, cool down (vt) | kühlen (vt) | ['ky:lən] |
| to chill (vi) | abkühlen (vi) | ['apky:lən] |

| taste, flavor | Geschmack (m) | ['gəʃmak] |
| aftertaste | Beigeschmack (m) | ['baɪgəʃmak] |

to be on a diet	auf Diät sein	['aɪnə di'ɛt zaɪn]
diet	Diät (f)	[di'et]
vitamin	Vitamin (n)	[wita'mi:n]
calorie	Kalorie (f)	[ka'lɔ:riə]

| vegetarian (n) | Vegetarier (m) | [wege'ta:riə] |
| vegetarian (adj) | vegetarisch | [wege'ta:riʃ] |

fats (nutrient)	Fett (n)	[fɛt]
proteins	Protein (n)	[prɔ'tɛi:n]
carbohydrates	Kohlehydrat (n)	['kɔ:ləhydrat]

slice (of lemon, ham)	Scheibchen (n)	['ʃaɪphən]
piece (of cake, pie)	Stück (n)	[ʃtyk]
crumb (of bread)	Krümel (m)	['kryml]

43. Table setting

spoon	Löffel (m)	['løfl]
knife	Messer (n)	['mɛsə]
fork	Gabel (f)	[ga:bl]

| cup (of coffee) | Tasse (f) | ['tasə] |
| plate (dinner ~) | Teller (m) | ['tɛlə] |

saucer	Untertasse (f)	['untər'tasə]
napkin (on table)	Serviette (f)	[zɛr'vjetə]
toothpick	Zahnstocher (m)	['ʦa:nʃtɔhə]

44. Restaurant

restaurant	**Restaurant** (n)	[rɛstɔ'ran]
coffee house	**Kaffeehaus** (n)	['kafe haus]
pub, bar	**Bar** (f)	[baːr]
tearoom	**Teesalon** (m)	['teːzaˈlɔːn]
waiter	**Kellner** (m)	['kɛlnə]
waitress	**Kellnerin** (f)	['kɛlnərin]
bartender	**Barmixer** (m)	['baːrmiksə]
menu	**Speisekarte** (f)	['ʃpaɪzəkartə]
wine list	**Weinkarte** (f)	['vaɪˈŋkartə]
to book a table	**einen Tisch reservieren**	['aɪnən tiʃ 'rezərwiːrən]
course, dish	**Gericht** (n)	['gəriħt]
to order (meal)	**bestellen** (vt)	['bəʃtɛlən]
to make an order	**eine Bestellung aufgeben**	['aɪnə 'bəʃtɛluŋ aʊfgeːbn]
aperitif	**Aperitif** (m)	[apəriˈtif]
appetizer	**Vorspeise** (f)	['foːrʃpaɪzə]
dessert	**Nachtisch** (m)	['naːhtiʃ]
check	**Rechnung** (f)	['rɛħnʊŋ]
to pay the check	**Rechnung bezahlen**	['rɛħnʊŋ 'bətsaːlən]
to give change	**das Wechselgeld geben**	[das 'vɛkselgəlt geːbn]
tip	**Trinkgeld** (n)	['triŋkgɛlt]

Family, relatives and friends

45. Personal information. Forms

name, first name	**Vorname** (m)	['fo:rna:mə]
family name	**Name** (m)	['na:mə]
date of birth	**Geburtsdatum** (n)	[gəbu:rtsda:tʊm]
place of birth	**Geburtsort** (m)	['gəbu:rtsɔrt]
nationality	**Nationalität** (f)	[natsi̯onali'tɛt]
place of residence	**Wohnort** (m)	['vo:n 'ɔrt]
country	**Staat** (m)	[ʃta:t]
profession (occupation)	**Beruf** (m)	['bəru:f]
gender, sex	**Geschlecht** (n)	['gəʃleht]
height	**Größe** (f)	['grøsə]
weight	**Gewicht** (n)	['gəwiht]

46. Family members. Relatives

mother	**Mutter** (f)	['mʊtə]
father	**Vater** (m)	['fa:tə]
son	**Sohn** (m)	[zo:n]
daughter	**Tochter** (f)	['tɔhtə]
younger daughter	**jüngste Tochter** (f)	['jʊŋstə 'tɔhtə]
younger son	**jüngste Sohn** (m)	['jʊŋstə 'zo:n]
eldest daughter	**ältere Tochter** (f)	['ɛltərə 'tɔhtə]
eldest son	**älterer Sohn** (m)	['ɛltərə 'zo:n]
brother	**Bruder** (m)	['bru:də]
sister	**Schwester** (f)	['ʃvɛstə]
cousin (masc.)	**Cousin** (m)	[kʊ'zɛn]
cousin (fem.)	**Cousine** (f)	[kʊ'zi:nə]
mom	**Mutter** (f)	['mʊtə]
dad, daddy	**Papa** (m)	[pa'pa:]
parents	**Eltern** (pl)	['ɛltərn]
child	**Kind** (n)	[kint]
children	**Kinder** (pl)	['kində]
grandmother	**Großmutter** (f)	['grɔsmʊtə]
grandfather	**Großvater** (m)	['grɔsfa:tə]
grandson	**Enkel** (m)	['ɛŋkl]

granddaughter	**Enkelin** (f)	['ɛŋkəlin]
grandchildren	**Enkelkinder** (pl)	['ɛŋkəl'kində]
uncle	**Onkel** (m)	['ɔŋkl]
aunt	**Tante** (f)	['tantə]
nephew	**Neffe** (m)	['nɛfə]
niece	**Nichte** (f)	['niĥtə]
mother-in-law (wife's mother)	**Schwiegermutter** (f)	['ʃwiːgəmʊtə]
father-in-law (husband's father)	**Schwiegervater** (m)	['ʃwiːgəfaːtə]
son-in-law (daughter's husband)	**Schwiegersohn** (m)	['ʃwiːgəzɔːn]
stepmother	**Stiefmutter** (f)	['ʃtiːfmʊtə]
stepfather	**Stiefvater** (m)	['ʃtiːfaːtə]
infant	**Säugling** (m)	['zɔɪgliŋ]
baby (infant)	**Kleinkind** (n)	['klaɪŋkint]
little boy, kid	**Kleine** (m)	['klaɪnə]
wife	**Frau** (f)	['frau]
husband	**Mann** (m)	[man]
spouse (husband)	**Ehemann** (m)	['eːə'man]
spouse (wife)	**Ehefrau** (f)	['eːəfrau]
married (masc.)	**verheiratet**	[fɛr'haɪraːtət]
married (fem.)	**verheiratet**	[fɛr'haɪraːtət]
single (unmarried)	**ledig**	['leːdiĥ]
bachelor	**Junggeselle** (m)	['jʊŋ ə'zɛlə]
divorced (masc.)	**geschieden**	['gəʃiːdən]
widow	**Witwe** (f)	['witvə]
widower	**Witwer** (m)	['witvə]
relative	**Verwandte** (m)	[fɛr'vantə]
close relative	**naher Verwandter** (m)	['naːə fɛr'vantə]
distant relative	**entfernter Verwandter** (m)	[ɛnt'fɛrntə fɛr'vantə]
relatives	**Verwandte** (pl)	[fɛr'vantə]
orphan (boy or girl)	**Waise** (f)	['vaɪzə]
guardian (of minor)	**Vormund** (m)	['foːr'mʊnt]
to adopt (a boy)	**adoptieren** (vt)	[adɔp'tiːrən]
to adopt (a girl)	**adoptieren** (vt)	[adɔp'tiːrən]

Medicine

47. Diseases

sickness	Krankheit (f)	['kraŋkhaɪt]
to be sick	krank sein	[kraŋk zaɪn]
health	Gesundheit (f)	['gəzunthaɪt]
runny nose (coryza)	Schnupfen (m)	['ʃnʊpfən]
angina	Angina (f)	[aŋ 'iːna]
cold (illness)	Erkältung (f)	[ɛr'kɛltʊŋ]
to catch a cold	sich erkälten	[ziħ ɛr'kɛltən]
bronchitis	Bronchitis (f)	[brɔn'hiːtis]
pneumonia	Lungenentzündung (f)	['luŋən ɛn'tsyndʊŋ]
flu, influenza	Grippe (f)	['gripə]
near-sighted (adj)	kurzsichtig	['kʊrtsziħtiħ]
far-sighted (adj)	weitsichtig	['vaɪtziħtiħ]
strabismus (crossed eyes)	Schielen (n)	['ʃiːlən]
cross-eyed (adj)	schielend	['ʃiːlənt]
cataract	grauer Star (m)	['grauə 'ʃtaːr]
glaucoma	Glaukom (n)	[glau'kɔːm]
stroke	Schlaganfall (m)	[ʃlaːk an'fal]
heart attack	Infarkt (m)	[in'farkt]
myocardial infarction	Herzinfarkt (m)	[hɛrts in'farkt]
paralysis	Lähmung (f)	['lɛːmʊŋ]
to paralyze (vt)	lähmen (vt)	['lɛmən]
allergy	Allergie (f)	[aler'giː]
asthma	Asthma (n)	['astma]
diabetes	Diabetes (m)	[di'abetɛs]
toothache	Zahnschmerz (m)	['tsaːnʃmɛrts]
caries	Karies (f)	['kariəs]
diarrhea	Durchfall (m)	['dʊrħfal]
constipation	Verstopfung (f)	[fɛrʃ'tɔpfʊŋ]
stomach upset	Magenverstimmung (f)	['maːgən fɛrʃ'timʊŋ]
food poisoning	Vergiftung (f)	[fɛr'giftʊŋ]
to have a food poisoning	sich vergiften	[ziħ fɛr'giftən]
arthritis	Arthritis (f)	[art'riːtis]
rickets	Rachitis (f)	[ra'hiːtis]
rheumatism	Rheumatismus (m)	[rɔɪma'tismʊs]

atherosclerosis	**Atherosklerose** (f)	['atərɔskle'rɔːzə]
gastritis	**Gastritis** (f)	[gast'riːtis]
appendicitis	**Blinddarmentzündung** (f)	['blintdarmɛnttsʏndʊŋ]
cholecystitis	**Cholezystitis** (f)	[hɔleʦis'tiːtis]
ulcer	**Geschwür** (n)	['gəʃwyr]

measles	**Masern** (pl)	['maːzərn]
German measles	**Röteln** (pl)	['røːtəln]
jaundice	**Gelbsucht** (f)	['gɛlpzuht]
hepatitis	**Hepatitis** (f)	[hɛpa'tiːtis]

schizophrenia	**Schizophrenie** (f)	[ʃitsofre'niː]
rabies (hydrophobia)	**Tollwut** (f)	['tɔlvuːt]
neurosis	**Neurose** (f)	[nɔɪ'rɔːzə]
concussion	**Gehirnerschütterung** (f)	['gəhirn 'ɛrʃytərʊŋ]

cancer	**Krebs** (m)	[kreːps]
sclerosis	**Sklerose** (f)	[skle'rɔːzə]
multiple sclerosis	**multiple Sklerose** (f)	[mʊl'tiple skle'rɔːzə]

alcoholism	**Alkoholismus** (m)	[alkɔhɔ'liːzmʊs]
alcoholic (n)	**Alkoholiker** (m)	[alkɔ'hoːlike]
syphilis	**Syphilis** (f)	['zyːfilis]
AIDS	**AIDS**	[ɛɪʦ]

tumor	**Tumor** (m)	['tuːmɔːr]
fever	**Fieber** (n)	['fiːbə]
malaria	**Malaria** (f)	[ma'laria]
gangrene	**Gangrän** (f, n)	[gaŋ 'rɛːn]
seasickness	**Seekrankheit** (f)	['zeːk'raŋkhaɪt]
epilepsy	**Epilepsie** (f)	[ɛpilep'siː]

epidemic	**Epidemie** (f)	[ɛpidə'miː]
typhus	**Typhus** (m)	['tyːfʊs]
tuberculosis	**Tuberkulose** (f)	[tʊbɐkʊ'løːzə]
cholera	**Cholera** (f)	[kɔ:'lera]
plague (bubonic ~)	**Pest** (f)	[pɛst]

48. Symptoms. Treatments. Part 1

symptom	**Symptom** (n)	[zymp'tɔːm]
temperature	**Temperatur** (f)	[tɛmpəra'tuːə]
high temperature	**Fieber** (n)	['fiːbə]
pulse	**Puls** (m)	[pʊls]

giddiness	**Schwindel** (m)	['ʃwindl]
hot (adj)	**heiß**	[haɪs]
shivering	**Schüttelfrost** (m)	['ʃytəlfrɔst]
pale (e.g., ~ face)	**blass**	[blas]
cough	**Husten** (m)	['hʊstən]

to cough (vi)	husten (vi)	['husten]
to sneeze (vi)	niesen (vi)	['ni:zen]
faint	Ohnmacht (f)	['ɔ:n'maht]
to faint (vi)	ohnmächtig werden	['ɔ:n'mahtiɦ 'we:rden]
bruise (hématome)	blauer Fleck (m)	['blaue 'flɛk]
bump (lump)	Beule (f)	['bɔilə]
to bruise oneself	sich stoßen	[ziɦ 'ʃtɔ:sen]
bruise (contusion)	Prellung (f)	['prɛluŋ]
to get bruised	eine Prellung zuziehen	['aine 'prɛluŋ 'tsuʦi:en]
to limp (vi)	hinken (vi)	['hiŋkən]
dislocation	Verrenkung (f)	[fɛ'rɛŋkuŋ]
to dislocate (vt)	ausrenken (vt)	['ausreŋken]
fracture	Fraktur (f)	[frak'tu:r]
to have a fracture	brechen (vt)	['brɛhn]
cut (e.g., paper ~)	Schnittwunde (f)	['ʃnitvunde]
to cut oneself	sich schneiden	[ziɦ 'ʃnaiden]
bleeding	Blutung (f)	['blu:tuŋ]
burn (injury)	Verbrennung (f)	[fɛrb'rɛnuŋ]
to scald oneself	sich verbrennen	[ziɦ fɛrb'rɛnen]
to prick (vt)	stechen (vt)	['ʃtɛhn]
to prick oneself	sich stechen	[ziɦ 'ʃtɛhn]
to injure (vt)	verletzen (vt)	[fɛr'letsen]
injury	Verletzung (f)	[fɛr'letsuŋ]
wound	Wunde (f)	['vunde]
trauma	Trauma (n)	['trauma]
to be delirious	irrereden (vi)	['irrere:den]
to stutter (vi)	stottern (vi)	['ʃtotern]
sunstroke	Sonnenstich (m)	['zonen ʃtiɦ]

49. Symptoms. Treatments. Part 2

pain	Schmerz (m)	[ʃmɛrts]
splinter (in foot, etc.)	Splitter (m)	['ʃplite]
sweat (perspiration)	Schweiß (m)	[ʃvais]
vomiting	Erbrechen (n)	[ɛrb'rɛhn]
convulsions	Krämpfe (pl)	['krɛmpfe]
pregnant (adj)	schwangere	['ʃvaŋere]
to be born	geboren sein	['gebɔ:ren zain]
delivery, labor	Geburt (f)	['gebu:rt]
to deliver (~ a baby)	gebären (vt)	['gebɛren]
abortion	Abtreibung (f)	['aptraibuŋ]
breathing, respiration	Atem (m)	['a:tem]

inhalation	Atemzug (m)	['atəmtsuk]
exhalation	Ausatmung (f)	['ausatmʊŋ]
to exhale (vi)	ausatmen (vt)	['ausatmən]
to inhale (vi)	einatmen (vt)	['aɪnatmən]

disabled person	Invalide (m)	[inva'li:də]
cripple	Krüppel (m)	['krypəl]
drug addict	Drogenabhängiger (m)	['drɔ:gən 'aphɛŋigə]

deaf (adj)	taub	['taup]
dumb, mute	stumm	[ʃtʊm]
deaf-and-dumb (adj)	taubstumm	['taupʃtʊm]

mad, insane (adj)	verrückt	[fɛ'rykt]
madman	Irre (m)	['irə]
madwoman	Irre (f)	['irə]
to go insane	den Verstand verlieren	[den fɛrʃtant fɛr'li:rən]

gene	Gen (n)	[gen]
immunity	Immunität (f)	[imʊni'tɛt]
hereditary (adj)	Erb-	[ɛrp]
congenital (adj)	angeboren	['aŋ ebɔ:rən]

virus	Virus (n)	['wi:rʊs]
microbe	Mikrobe (f)	[mik'rɔ:bə]
bacterium	Bakterie (f)	[bak'tɛriə]
infection	Infektion (f)	[infɛk'tsʲɔ:n]

50. Symptoms. Treatments. Part 3

| hospital | Krankenhaus (n) | ['kraŋkən haus] |
| patient | Patient (m) | [patsi'ɛnt] |

diagnosis	Diagnose (f)	[diag'nɔ:zə]
cure	Heilung (f)	['haɪlʊŋ]
medical treatment	Behandlung (f)	['bəhandlʊŋ]
to get treatment	Behandlung bekommen	['bəhandlʊŋ 'bekɔ:mən]
to treat (vt)	pflegen (vt)	['pfle:gən]
to nurse (look after)	pflegen (vt)	['pfle:gən]
care (nursing ~)	Pflege (f)	['pfle:gə]

operation, surgery	Operation (f)	[ɔpəra'tsʲɔ:n]
to bandage (head, limb)	verbinden (vt)	[fɛr'bindən]
bandaging	Verband (m)	[fɛr'bant]

vaccination	Impfung (f)	['impfʊŋ]
to vaccinate (vt)	impfen (vt)	['impfən]
injection, shot	Spritze (f)	['ʃpritsə]
to give an injection	eine Spritze geben	['aɪnə 'ʃpritsə ge:bn]
attack	Anfall (m)	['anfal]

amputation	Amputation (f)	[ampʊtaˈtsˈɔːn]
to amputate (vt)	amputieren (vt)	[ampʊˈtiːrən]
coma	Koma (n)	[ˈkɔːma]
to be in a coma	im Koma liegen	[im ˈkɔːma ˈliːgən]
intensive care	Reanimation (f)	[reanimaˈtsˈɔːn]

to recover (~ from flu)	genesen von ...	[ˈgəneːzən fɔn]
state (patient's ~)	Zustand (m)	[ˈtsuːʃtant]
consciousness	Bewusstsein (n)	[ˈbəvʊstzaɪn]
memory (faculty)	Gedächtnis (n)	[ˈgədɛhtnis]

to extract (tooth)	ziehen (vt)	[ˈtsiːən]
filling	Plombe (f)	[ˈplømbə]
to fill (a tooth)	plombieren (vt)	[plɔmˈbiːrən]

| hypnosis | Hypnose (f) | [hypˈnɔːzə] |
| to hypnotize (vt) | hypnotisieren (vt) | [hypnotiˈziːrən] |

51. Doctors

doctor	Arzt (m)	[aːrtst]
nurse	Krankenschwester (f)	[ˈkraŋkən ˈʃvɛstə]
private physician	Privatarzt (m)	[priˈvaːt ˈaːrtst]

dentist	Zahnarzt (m)	[tsaːn ˈaːrtst]
ophthalmologist	Augenarzt (m)	[ˈaugən ˈaːrtst]
internist	Internist (m)	[intərˈnist]
surgeon	Chirurg (m)	[hiˈrʊrk]

psychiatrist	Psychiater (m)	[psyhiˈatə]
pediatrician	Kinderarzt (m)	[ˈkindər ˈaːrtst]
psychologist	Psychologe (m)	[psyhɔˈlɔːgə]
gynecologist	Frauenarzt (m)	[ˈfrauən aːrtst]
cardiologist	Kardiologe (m)	[kardiɔˈlɔːgə]

52. Medicine. Drugs. Accessories

medicine, drug	Arznei (f)	[artsˈnaɪ]
remedy	Heilmittel (n)	[ˈhaɪlˈmitl]
to prescribe (vt)	verschreiben (vt)	[fɛrʃˈraɪbn]
prescription	Rezept (n)	[reˈtsɛpt]

tablet, pill	Tablette (f)	[tabˈletə]
ointment	Salbe (f)	[ˈzalbə]
ampule	Ampulle (f)	[amˈpʊlə]
mixture	Mixtur (f)	[miksˈtʊːr]
syrup	Sirup (m)	[ziˈrʊp]
pill	Pille (f)	[ˈpilə]

powder	**Pulver** (n)	['pʊlvə]
bandage	**Verband** (m)	[fɛr'bant]
cotton wool	**Watte** (f)	['vatə]
iodine	**Jod** (n)	[jɔt]
Band-Aid	**Pflaster** (n)	['pflastə]
eyedropper	**Pipette** (f)	[pi'petə]
thermometer	**Thermometer** (n)	[tɛrmɔ'meːtə]
syringe	**Spritze** (f)	['ʃpritsə]
wheelchair	**Rollstuhl** (m)	['rɔlʃtuːl]
crutches	**Krücken** (pl)	['krykən]
painkiller	**Betäubungsmittel** (n)	['bətɔɪbʊŋsmitl]
laxative	**Abführmittel** (n)	['apfyːr'mitl]
spirit (ethanol)	**Spiritus** (m)	['ʃpiːritʊs]
medicinal herbs	**Heilkraut** (n)	['haɪlk'raut]
herbal (~ tea)	**Kräuter-**	['krɔɪtə]

HUMAN HABITAT

City

53. City. Life in the city

city, town	**Stadt** (f)	[ʃtat]
capital city	**Hauptstadt** (f)	[ˈhauptʃtat]
village	**Dorf** (n)	[dɔrf]
city map	**Stadtplan** (m)	[ˈʃtatplan]
downtown	**Stadtzentrum** (n)	[ʃtat ˈʦɛntrʊm]
suburb	**Vorort** (m)	[fɔːr ˈɔrt]
suburban (adj)	**Vorort-**	[fɔːr ˈɔrt]
outskirts	**Stadtrand** (m)	[ˈʃtatrant]
environs (suburbs)	**Umgebung** (f)	[umˈgeːbʊŋ]
city block	**Stadtviertel** (n)	[ˈʃtatfirtl]
residential block	**Wohnblock** (m)	[ˈvoːnblɔk]
traffic	**Straßenverkehr** (m)	[ˈʃtrasən fɛrˈkeːr]
traffic lights	**Ampel** (f)	[ˈampl]
public transportation	**Stadtverkehr** (m)	[ˈʃtatfɛrkeːr]
intersection	**Straßenkreuzung** (f)	[ˈʃtrasən ˈkrɔɪʦuŋ]
crosswalk	**Übergang** (m)	[ˈjuːbərɡaŋ]
pedestrian underpass	**Fußgängerunterführung**	[ˈfuːsgɛŋər ˈuntərfyːrʊn]
to cross (vt)	**überqueren** (vt)	[juːbərkˈvɛrən]
pedestrian	**Fußgänger** (m)	[ˈfuːsgɛŋə]
sidewalk	**Gehweg** (m)	[ˈgeːəweːk]
bridge	**Brücke** (f)	[ˈbrykə]
bank (riverbank)	**Kai** (m)	[kaɪ]
allée	**Allee** (f)	[aˈleː]
park	**Park** (m)	[park]
boulevard	**Boulevard** (m)	[bʊlˈvaːr]
square	**Platz** (m)	[plaʦ]
avenue (wide street)	**Prospekt** (m)	[prɔsˈpɛkt]
street	**Straße** (f)	[ˈʃtrasə]
side street	**Gasse** (f)	[ˈgasə]
dead end	**Sackgasse** (f)	[ˈzakgasə]
house	**Haus** (n)	[ˈhaus]
building	**Gebäude** (n)	[ˈɡəbɔɪdə]

skyscraper	Wolkenkratzer (m)	['vɔlkəŋk'ratsə]
facade	Fassade (f)	[fa'sadə]
roof	Dach (n)	[dah]
window	Fenster (n)	['fɛnstə]
arch	Bogen (m)	['boːgən]
column	Säule (f)	['zɔɪlə]
corner	Ecke (f)	['ɛkə]

store window	Schaufenster (n)	[ʃau'fɛnstə]
store sign	Schild (n)	[ʃilt]
poster	Anschlag (m)	['anʃlaːk]
advertising poster	Werbeposter (m)	['vɛrbə'postə]
billboard	Werbeschild (n)	['vɛrbəʃilt]

garbage, trash	Müll (m)	[myl]
garbage can	Mülleimer (m)	['my'laɪmə]
to litter (vi)	Abfall wegwerfen	['apfal wek'werfən]
garbage dump	Mülldeponie (f)	['myldepɔniː]

phone booth	Telefonzelle (f)	['teːləfɔːn 'tsɛlə]
lamppost	Straßenlaterne (f)	['ʃtrasən la'tɛrnə]
bench (park ~)	Bank (f)	[baŋk]

police officer	Polizist (m)	[poli'tsist]
police	Polizei (f)	[poli'tsaɪ]
beggar	Bettler (m)	['bɛtlə]
homeless, bum	Obdachlose (m)	['ɔpdahlɔːzə]

54. Urban institutions

store	Laden (m)	['laːdən]
drugstore, pharmacy	Apotheke (f)	[apo'teːkə]
optical store	Optik (f)	['ɔptik]
shopping mall	Einkaufszentrum (n)	['aɪnkaufs 'tsɛntrʊm]
supermarket	Supermarkt (m)	['zupərmarkt]

bakery	Bäckerei (f)	[bəke'raɪ]
baker	Bäcker (m)	['bɛkə]
candy store	Konditorei (f)	[kɔndito'raɪ]
grocery store	Lebensmittelladen (m)	['leːbəns 'mitəl'laːdən]
butcher shop	Metzgerei (f)	[mɛtsge'raɪ]

| produce store | Gemüseladen (m) | ['gəmyːzə 'laːdən] |
| market | Markt (m) | [markt] |

coffee house	Kaffeehaus (n)	['kafe haus]
restaurant	Restaurant (n)	[rɛsto'ran]
pub	Bierstube (f)	['biːrʃtuːbə]
pizzeria	Pizzeria (f)	[pitsɛria]
hair salon	Friseursalon (m)	[fri'zøːr za'lɔːn]

post office	**Post** (f)	[pɔst]
dry cleaners	**chemische Reinigung** (f)	['heːmiʃə 'raɪnɪgʊŋ]
photo studio	**Fotoatelier** (n)	['fɔtɔate'ʎje]

shoe store	**Schuhgeschäft** (n)	['ʃuːgəʃɛft]
bookstore	**Buchhandlung** (f)	['buhandlʊŋ]
sporting goods store	**Sportladen** (m)	['ʃpɔrtlaːdən]

clothes repair	**Kleiderreparatur** (f)	['klaɪdə rəpara'tuːr]
formal wear rental	**Bekleidungsverleih** (m)	['bəklaɪdʊŋs fɛr'laɪ]
movie rental store	**Filmverleih** (m)	['filmfɛr'laɪ]

circus	**Zirkus** (m)	['tsɪrkʊs]
zoo	**Zoo** (m)	['tsɔː]
movie theater	**Kino** (n)	['kiːnɔ]
museum	**Museum** (n)	[mʊ'zɛum]
library	**Bibliothek** (f)	[biblio'teːk]

| theater | **Theater** (n) | [te'aːtə] |
| opera | **Opernhaus** (n) | ['ɔpərnhaus] |

| nightclub | **Nachtklub** (m) | ['nahtklup] |
| casino | **Kasino** (n) | [ka'ziːnɔ] |

mosque	**Moschee** (f)	[mɔ'ʃɛː]
synagogue	**Synagoge** (f)	[zyna'gɔːgə]
cathedral	**Kathedrale** (f)	[kated'raːlə]

| temple | **Tempel** (m) | ['tɛmpl] |
| church | **Kirche** (f) | ['kirhə] |

college	**Institut** (n)	[insti'tʊt]
university	**Universität** (f)	[univɛrzi'tɛːt]
school	**Schule** (f)	['ʃuːlə]

| prefecture | **Präfektur** (f) | [prɛfək'tuːr] |
| city hall | **Rathaus** (n) | ['rathaus] |

| hotel | **Hotel** (n) | [hɔ'tɛl] |
| bank | **Bank** (f) | [baŋk] |

| embassy | **Botschaft** (f) | ['bɔːtʃaft] |
| travel agency | **Reisebüro** (n) | [raɪzəby'rɔː] |

| information office | **Informationsbüro** (n) | [infɔrma'tsɔːns by'rɔː] |
| money exchange | **Wechselstelle** (f) | ['vɛksəlʃtɛlə] |

| subway | **U-Bahn** (f) | ['uːbaːn] |
| hospital | **Krankenhaus** (n) | ['kraŋkən haus] |

| gas station | **Tankstelle** (f) | ['taŋkʃtɛlə] |
| parking lot | **Parkstelle** (f) | ['parkʃtələ] |

55. Signs

store sign	**Schild** (n)	[ʃɪlt]
notice (written text)	**Aufschrift** (f)	[ˈaʊfʃrɪft]
poster	**Plakat** (n)	[plaˈkaːt]
direction sign	**Wegeweiser** (m)	[ˈveːgevaɪzə]
arrow (sign)	**Pfeil** (m)	[pfaɪl]
caution	**Vorsicht** (f)	[ˈfɔːzɪht]
warning sign	**Warnung** (f)	[ˈvarnʊŋ]
to warn (vt)	**warnen** (vt)	[ˈvarnən]
day off	**freier Tag** (m)	[ˈfraɪə taːk]
timetable (schedule)	**Plan** (m)	[plaːn]
opening hours	**Öffnungszeiten** (pl)	[øfnʊŋs ˈtsaɪtən]
WELCOME!	**HERZLICH WILLKOMMEN!**	[ˈhɛrtslɪh wilˈkɔmən]
ENTRANCE	**EINGANG**	[ˈaɪŋ aŋ]
EXIT	**AUSGANG**	[ˈausgaŋ]
PUSH	**DRÜCKEN**	[ˈdrykən]
PULL	**ZIEHEN**	[ˈtsiːən]
OPEN	**GEÖFFNET**	[gəøfnət]
CLOSED	**GESCHLOSSEN**	[ˈgəʃlɔsn]
WOMEN	**DAMEN, FRAUEN**	[ˈdamən], [ˈfrauən]
MEN	**HERREN, MÄNNER**	[hɛrrən], [ˈmɛnə]
DISCOUNTS	**AUSVERKAUF**	[ausfɛrˈkauf]
SALE	**REDUZIERT**	[reduˈtsirt]
NEW!	**NEU!**	[nɔɪ]
FREE	**GRATIS**	[ˈgraːtis]
ATTENTION!	**ACHTUNG!**	[ˈahtʊŋ]
NO VACANCIES	**ZIMMER BELEGT**	[ˈtsimə ˈbəligt]
RESERVED	**RESERVIERT**	[rezərˈwiːrt]
ADMINISTRATION	**VERWALTUNG**	[fɛrˈvaltʊŋ]
STAFF ONLY	**NUR FÜR PERSONAL**	[nuːr fyr pɛrzɔˈnaːl]
BEWARE OF THE DOG!	**VORSICHT BISSIGER HUND**	[ˈfɔːzɪht ˈbisigə hʊnt]
NO SMOKING	**RAUCHEN VERBOTEN!**	[ˈrauhən fɛrˈbɔːtən]
DO NOT TOUCH!	**BITTE NICHT BERÜHREN**	[ˈbitə niht bəˈryːrən]
DANGEROUS	**GEFÄHRLICH**	[ˈgəfɛːrlih]
DANGER	**VORSICHT!**	[ˈfɔːzɪht]
HIGH TENSION	**HOCHSPANNUNG**	[ˈhɔhʃpanʊŋ]
NO SWIMMING!	**BADEN VERBOTEN**	[ˈbaːdən fɛrˈbɔːtən]

OUT OF ORDER	**AUßER BETRIEB**	['ausə 'betriːp]
FLAMMABLE	**LEICHTENTZÜNDLICH**	['laıҺt ɛn'ʦyndliҺ]
FORBIDDEN	**VERBOTEN**	[fɛr'boːtən]
NO TRESPASSING!	**DURCHGANG**	['dʊrҺgaŋ
	VERBOTEN	fɛr'boːtən]
WET PAINT	**FRISCH GESTRICHEN**	[friʃ 'gəʃtriːhn]

56. Urban transportation

bus	**Bus** (m)	[hʊs]
streetcar	**Straßenbahn** (f)	['ʃtrasən 'baːn]
trolley	**Obus** (m)	['ɔːbʊs]
route (of bus)	**Linie** (f)	['liːniə]
number (e.g., bus ~)	**Nummer** (f)	['nʊmə]
to go by ...	**mit ... fahren**	[mit 'faːrən]
to get on (~ the bus)	**einsteigen** (vi)	['aınʃtaıgən]
to get off ...	**aussteigen** (vi)	['ausʃtaıgən]
stop (e.g., bus ~)	**Haltestelle** (f)	['haltəʃtələ]
next stop	**nächste Haltestelle** (f)	['nɛkstə 'haltəʃtələ]
terminus	**Endhaltestelle** (f)	['ɛnthaltəʃtələ]
schedule	**Fahrplan** (m)	['faːrplaːn]
to wait (vt)	**warten** (vi, vt)	['vartən]
ticket	**Fahrkarte** (f)	['faːrkartə]
fare	**Fahrpreis** (m)	['faːrpraıs]
cashier (ticket seller)	**Kassierer** (m)	[ka'siːrə]
ticket inspection	**Fahrkartenkontrolle** (f)	['faːrkartən kont'rɔːlə]
conductor	**Kontrolleur** (m)	[kɔntrɔ'løːr]
to be late (for ...)	**sich verspäten**	[ziҺ fɛrʃ'pɛːtən]
to miss (~ the train, etc.)	**versäumen** (vt)	[fɛr'zɔımən]
to be in a hurry	**sich beeilen**	[ziҺ 'bəaılən]
taxi, cab	**Taxi** (n)	['taksi]
taxi driver	**Taxifahrer** (m)	['taksifaːrə]
by taxi	**mit dem Taxi**	[mit dem 'taksi]
taxi stand	**Taxistand** (m)	['taksiʃtant]
to call a taxi	**ein Taxi bestellen**	[aın 'taksi 'bəʃtɛlən]
to take a taxi	**ein Taxi nehmen**	[aın 'taksi 'neːmən]
traffic	**Straßenverkehr** (m)	['ʃtrasən fɛr'keːr]
traffic jam	**Stau** (m)	['ʃtau]
rush hour	**Hauptverkehrszeit** (f)	['hauptfɛr'keːrs 'ʦaıt]
to park (vi)	**parken** (vi)	['parkən]
to park (vt)	**parken** (vt)	['parkən]
parking lot	**Parkplatz** (m)	['paːrkplaʦ]
subway	**U-Bahn** (f)	['uːbaːn]

station	**Station** (f)	[ʃta'ts'o:n]
to take the subway	**mit der U-Bahn fahren**	[mit də 'u:ba:n 'fa:rən]
train	**Zug** (m)	[tsuk]
train station	**Bahnhof** (m)	['ba:nhɔf]

57. Sightseeing

monument	**Denkmal** (n)	['dɛŋkma:l]
fortress	**Festung** (f)	['fɛstuŋ]
palace	**Palast** (m)	[pa'last]
castle	**Schloss** (n)	[ʃlɔs]
tower	**Turm** (m)	[turm]
mausoleum	**Mausoleum** (n)	[mavzɔ'leum]
architecture	**Architektur** (f)	[arhitɛk'tu:r]
medieval (adj)	**mittelalterlich**	['mitl 'altərliɦ]
ancient (adj)	**alt**	[alt]
national (adj)	**national**	[nats'o'na:l]
well-known (adj)	**berühmt**	['bərymt]
tourist	**Tourist** (m)	[tu'rist]
guide (person)	**Fremdenführer** (m)	['frɛmdən 'fy:rə]
excursion, guided tour	**Ausflug** (m)	['ausflu:k]
to show (vt)	**zeigen** (vt)	['tsaigən]
to tell (vt)	**erzählen** (vt)	[ɛr'tsɛlən]
to find (vt)	**finden** (vt)	['findən]
to get lost (lose one's way)	**sich verlieren**	[ziɦ fɛr'li:rən]
map (e.g., subway ~)	**Karte** (f)	['kartə]
map (e.g., city ~)	**Karte** (f)	['kartə]
souvenir, gift	**Souvenir** (n)	[zuvə'ni:r]
gift shop	**Souvenirladen** (m)	[zuvə'ni:r'la:dən]
to take pictures	**fotografieren** (vt)	[fɔtɔgra'fi:rən]
to be photographed	**sich fotografieren**	[ziɦ fɔtɔgra'fi:rən]

58. Shopping

to buy (purchase)	**kaufen** (vt)	['kaufən]
purchase	**Einkauf** (m)	['aiŋkauf]
to go shopping	**einkaufen gehen**	['aiŋkaufən 'ge:ən]
shopping	**Einkaufen** (n)	['aiŋkaufən]
to be open (ab. store)	**offen sein**	['ɔfən zain]
to be closed	**zu sein**	[tsu zain]
footwear	**Schuhe** (pl)	['ʃu:ə]
clothes, clothing	**Kleidung** (f)	['klaiduŋ]

cosmetics	Kosmetik (f)	[kɔs'me:tik]
food products	Lebensmittel (pl)	['le:bəns 'mitəl]
gift, present	Geschenk (n)	['gəʃɛŋk]

| salesman | Verkäufer (m) | [fɛr'kɔɪfə] |
| saleswoman | Verkäuferin (f) | [fɛr'kɔɪfɛrin] |

check out, cash desk	Kasse (f)	['kasə]
mirror	Spiegel (m)	['ʃpi:gl]
counter (in shop)	Ladentisch (m)	['la:dəntiʃ]
fitting room	Umkleidekabine (f)	['umklaɪdə ka'bi:nə]

to try on	anprobieren (vt)	['anprɔbi:rən]
to fit (ab. dress, etc.)	passen (vi)	['pasn]
to like (I like ...)	gefallen (vi)	['gəfalən]

price	Preis (m)	[praɪs]
price tag	Preisschild (n)	['praɪsʃilt]
to cost (vt)	kosten (vt)	['kɔstən]
How much?	Wie viel?	['wi:fi:l]
discount	Rabatt (m)	[ra'bat]

inexpensive (adj)	preiswert	['praɪsvərt]
cheap (adj)	billig	['biliħ]
expensive (adj)	teuer	['tɔɪə]
It's expensive	Das ist teuer	[das ist 'tɔɪə]

rental (n)	Verleih (m)	[fɛr'laɪ]
to rent (~ a tuxedo)	ausleihen (vt)	['ausla:ən]
credit	Kredit (m)	[kre'di:t]
on credit (adv)	auf Kredit	['auf kre'di:t]

59. Money

money	Geld (n)	[gəlt]
currency exchange	Austausch (m)	['austauʃ]
exchange rate	Kurs (m)	[kʊrs]
ATM	Geldautomat (m)	['gɛlt autɔ'ma:t]
coin	Münze (f)	['myntsə]

| dollar | Dollar (m) | ['dɔlar] |
| euro | Euro (m) | ['ɔɪrɔ] |

lira	Lira (f)	['li:ra]
Deutschmark	Mark (f)	[mark]
franc	Franken (m)	[fraŋkən]
pound sterling	Pfund Sterling (n)	['pfʊnt 'ʃtɛrliŋ]
yen	Yen (m)	[jen]
debt	Schuld (f)	[ʃʊlt]
debtor	Schuldner (m)	['ʃʊldnə]

| to lend (money) | leihen (vt) | ['la:ɪən] |
| to borrow (vi, vt) | ausleihen (vt) | ['ausla:ən] |

bank	Bank (f)	[baŋk]
account	Konto (n)	['kɔntɔ]
to deposit (vt)	einzahlen (vt)	['aɪntsa:lən]
to withdraw (vt)	abheben (vt)	['aphe:bn]

credit card	Kreditkarte (f)	[kre'di:t 'kartə]
cash	Bargeld (n)	['bargəlt]
check	Scheck (m)	[ʃɛk]
to write a check	einen Scheck schreiben	['aɪnən ʃɛk 'ʃraɪbn]
checkbook	Scheckbuch (n)	['ʃɛkbʊh]

wallet	Geldtasche (f)	['gɛltaʃə]
change purse	Geldbeutel (m)	['gɛlt bɔɪtl]
billfold	Brieftasche (f)	['briftaʃə]
safe	Safe (m)	[sɛɪf]

heir	Erbe (m)	['ɛrbə]
inheritance	Erbschaft (n)	['ɛrpʃaft]
fortune (wealth)	Vermögen (n)	[fɛr'mø:gən]

lease, rent	Pacht (f)	[paht]
rent money	Miete (f)	['mi:tə]
to rent (sth from sb)	mieten (vt)	['mi:tən]

price	Preis (m)	[praɪs]
cost	Kosten (pl)	['kɔstən]
sum	Summe (f)	['zumə]

to spend (vt)	ausgeben (vt)	['ausge:bn]
expenses	Ausgaben (pl)	['ausga:bn]
to economize (vi, vt)	sparen (vt)	['ʃpa:rən]
economical	sparsam	['ʃpa:rzam]

to pay (vi, vt)	zahlen (vt)	['tsa:lən]
payment	Lohn (m)	[lɔ:n]
change (give the ~)	Wechselgeld (n)	['vɛksəl'gelt]

tax	Steuer (f)	['ʃtɔɪə]
fine	Geldstrafe (f)	['gɛlt 'ʃtra:fə]
to fine (vt)	bestrafen (vt)	['bəʃtra:fən]

60. Post. Postal service

post office	Post (f)	[pɔst]
mail (letters, etc.)	Post (f)	[pɔst]
mailman	Briefträger (m)	['bri:ftrəgə]
opening hours	Öffnungszeiten (pl)	[øfnʊŋs 'tsaɪtən]

letter	**Brief** (m)	[bri:f]
registered letter	**Einschreibebrief** (m)	[ˈaɪnʃraɪbə bri:f]
postcard	**Postkarte** (f)	[ˈpɔstkartə]
telegram	**Telegramm** (n)	[teleɡˈram]
parcel	**Postpaket** (n)	[pɔstpaˈke:t]
money transfer	**Geldanweisung** (f)	[ˈɡɛlt anˈvaɪzuŋ]

to receive (vt)	**bekommen** (vt)	[ˈbəkɔmən]
to send (vt)	**abschicken** (vt)	[ˈapʃikən]
sending	**Absendung** (f)	[ˈapzənduŋ]

address	**Postanschrift** (f)	[ˈpɔst anʃrift]
ZIP code	**Postleitzahl** (f)	[ˈpɔstlaɪtsa:l]
sender	**Absender** (m)	[ˈapzəndə]
receiver, addressee	**Empfänger** (m)	[ɛmpˈfɛŋə]

name	**Vorname** (m)	[ˈfɔːrna:mə]
family name	**Nachname** (m)	[ˈna:hˈna:mə]

rate (of postage)	**Tarif** (m)	[taˈrif]
standard (adj)	**Standard-**	[ˈʃtandart]
economical (adj)	**Spar-**	[ʃpa]

weight	**Gewicht** (n)	[ˈɡəwiht]
to weigh up (vt)	**abwiegen** (vt)	[ˈapwi:ɡən]
envelope	**Briefumschlag** (m)	[ˈbri:f ˈumʃla:k]
postage stamp	**Briefmarke** (f)	[ˈbrifmarkə]
to stamp an envelope	**Briefmarke aufkleben**	[ˈbrifmarkə ˈaufkle:bn]

Dwelling. House. Home

61. House. Electricity

electricity	Elektrizität (f)	[ɛlektritsi'tɛt]
light bulb	Glühbirne (f)	['gly:birnə]
switch	Schalter (m)	['ʃaltə]
fuse	Sicherung (f)	['ziherʊŋ]
cable, wire (electric ~)	Draht (m)	[dra:t]
wiring	Leitung (f)	['laitʊŋ]
electricity meter	Stromzähler (m)	['ʃtrɔ:mtsɛlə]
readings	Anzeige (f)	['antsaigə]

62. Villa. Mansion

country house	Landhaus (n)	['lanthaus]
villa (by sea)	Villa (f)	['wila]
wing (of building)	Flügel (m)	['fly:gl]
garden	Garten (m)	['gartən]
park	Park (m)	[park]
tropical greenhouse	Orangerie (f)	[ɔranʒə'ri:]
to look after (garden, etc.)	pflegen (vt)	['pfle:gən]
swimming pool	Schwimmbad (n)	['ʃwimbat]
gym	Kraftraum (m)	['kraftraum]
tennis court	Tennisplatz (m)	['tɛnisplats]
home theater room	Heimkinoraum (m)	[haim 'kino 'raum]
garage	Garage (f)	[ga'ra:ʒə]
private property	Privateigentum (n)	[pri'va:t 'aigntʊ:m]
private land	Privatgrundstück (n)	[pri'va:t 'grʊntʃtyk]
warning (caution)	Warnung (f)	['varnʊŋ]
warning sign	Warnschild (n)	['varn'ʃilt]
security	Bewachung (f)	['bəvahʊŋ]
security guard	Wächter (m)	['vɛhtə]
burglar alarm	Alarmanlage (f)	[ala:rmən'lagə]

63. Apartment

apartment	Wohnung (f)	['vɔːnʊŋ]
room	Zimmer (n)	['tsimə]
bedroom	Schlafzimmer (n)	['ʃlaːftsimə]
dining room	Esszimmer (n)	['ɛs'tsimə]
living room	Wohnzimmer (n)	['vɔːn'tsimə]
study (home office)	Arbeitszimmer (n)	['arbaɪts 'tsimə]
entry room	Vorzimmer (n)	['fortsimə]
bathroom	Badezimmer (n)	['baːdə'tsimə]
half bath	Toilette (f)	[toa'letə]
ceiling	Decke (f)	['dɛkə]
floor	Fußboden (m)	['fuːsbɔːdən]
corner	Ecke (f)	['ɛkə]

64. Furniture. Interior

furniture	Möbel (n)	['møːbl]
table	Tisch (m)	[tiʃ]
chair	Stuhl (m)	[ʃtuːl]
bed	Bett (n)	[bət]
couch, sofa	Sofa (n)	['zɔːfa]
armchair	Sessel (m)	['zɛsl]
bookcase	Bücherschrank (m)	['byhərʃraŋk]
shelf	Regal (n)	[re'gaːl]
set of shelves	Etagere (f)	[ɛta'ʒeːrə]
wardrobe	Schrank (m)	[ʃraŋk]
coat rack	Kleiderhakenleiste (f)	['klaɪdə 'hakən'laɪstə]
coat stand	Kleiderständer (m)	['klaɪdə 'ʃtɛndə]
dresser	Kommode (f)	[kɔ'mɔːdə]
coffee table	Couchtisch (m)	['kautʃtiʃ]
mirror	Spiegel (m)	['ʃpiːgl]
carpet	Teppich (m)	['tɛpih]
rug, small carpet	kleiner Teppich (m)	['klaɪnə 'tɛpih]
fireplace	Kamin (m, n)	[ka'min]
candle	Kerze (f)	['kɛrtsə]
candlestick	Kerzenleuchter (m)	['kɛrtsənløɪhtə]
drapes	Vorhänge (pl)	['fɔːrhɛŋə]
wallpaper	Tapete (f)	[ta'petə]
blinds (jalousie)	Jalousie (f)	[ʒaly'ziː]
table lamp	Tischlampe (f)	['tiʃlampə]

wall lamp (sconce)	Leuchte (f)	['løɪħtə]
floor lamp	Stehlampe (f)	['ʃte:lampə]
chandelier	Kronleuchter (m)	['krɔnløɪħtə]

leg (of chair, table)	Bein (n)	[baɪn]
armrest	Armlehne (f)	['arm'le:nə]
back (backrest)	Lehne (f)	['le:nə]
drawer	Schublade (f)	['ʃʊpla:də]

65. Bedding

bedclothes	Bettwäsche (f)	['bɛtvəʃə]
pillow	Kissen (n)	['kisn]
pillowcase	Kissenbezug (m)	['kisnbə'tsuk]
blanket (comforter)	Bettdecke (f)	['bɛtdəkə]
sheet	Laken (n)	['la:kən]
bedspread	Tagesdecke (f)	['ta:gəs 'dɛkə]

66. Kitchen

kitchen	Küche (f)	['kyhə]
gas	Gas (n)	[ga:s]
gas cooker	Gasherd (m)	[ga:s'he:rt]
electric cooker	Elektroherd (m)	[ɛ'lektrɔ'he:rt]
oven	Backofen (m)	['bakɔ:fən]
microwave oven	Mikrowellenherd (m)	[mikrɔ'vɛlen'hɛrt]

refrigerator	Kühlschrank (m)	['ky:lʃraŋk]
freezer	Tiefkühltruhe (f)	['tifkylt'ru:ə]
dishwasher	Geschirrspülmaschine (f)	['gəʃirʃpylmaʃi:nə]

meat grinder	Fleischwolf (m)	['flaɪʃvɔlf]
juicer	Saftpresse (f)	['zaftprɛsə]
toaster	Toaster (m)	['tɔstə]
mixer	Mixer (m)	['miksə]

coffee maker	Kaffeemaschine (f)	['kafe ma'ʃi:nə]
coffee pot	Kaffeekanne (f)	['kafe 'kanə]
coffee grinder	Kaffeemühle (f)	['kafe 'my:lə]

kettle	Wasserkessel (m)	['vasə'ke:sl]
teapot	Teekanne (f)	['te:'kanə]
lid	Deckel (m)	['dɛkl]
tea strainer	Teesieb (n)	['te:'zi:p]

spoon	Löffel (m)	['løfl]
teaspoon	Teelöffel (m)	['te:løfl]
tablespoon	Esslöffel (m)	['ɛsløfl]

fork	**Gabel** (f)	[ga:bl]
knife	**Messer** (n)	['mɛsə]
tableware (dishes)	**Geschirr** (n)	['gəʃir]
plate (dinner ~)	**Teller** (m)	['tɛlə]
saucer	**Untertasse** (f)	['untər'tasə]
shot glass	**Weinglas** (n)	['vaɪŋ la:s]
glass (~ of water)	**Glas** (n)	[gla:s]
cup	**Tasse** (f)	['tasə]
sugar bowl	**Zu̶ ̶krdose** (f)	['tsukər'dɔ:zə]
salt shaker	**Salzstreuer** (m)	['zaltsʃt'roɪə]
pepper shaker	**Pfefferstreuer** (m)	['pfɛfərʃtrɔɪə]
butter dish	**Butterdose** (f)	['butər'dɔ:zə]
saucepan	**Kochtopf** (m)	['kɔhtɔpf]
frying pan	**Pfanne** (f)	['pfanə]
ladle	**Schöpflöffel** (m)	['ʃɔpf'løfl]
colander	**Durchschlag** (m)	['durhʃ'la:k]
tray	**Tablett** (n)	[tab'let]
bottle	**Flasche** (f)	['fla:ʃə]
jar (glass)	**Einmachglas** (n)	[aɪnmahg'la:s]
can	**Dose** (f)	['dɔ:zə]
bottle opener	**Flaschenöffner** (m)	[flaʃən øfnə]
can opener	**Dosenöffner** (m)	['dɔ:zən øfnə]
corkscrew	**Korkenzieher** (m)	['korken'tsi:ə]
filter	**Filter** (n)	['filtə]
to filter (vt)	**filtern** (vt)	['filtərn]
trash	**Müll** (m)	[myl]
trash can	**Mülleimer** (m)	['my'laɪmə]

67. Bathroom

bathroom	**Badezimmer** (n)	['ba:də'tsimə]
water	**Wasser** (n)	['vasə]
tap, faucet	**Wasserhahn** (m)	['vasə'ha:n]
hot water	**Warmwasser** (n)	['varm'vasə]
cold water	**kaltes Wasser** (n)	['kaltəs 'vasə]
toothpaste	**Zahnpasta** (f)	['tsa:n'pasta]
to brush one's teeth	**Zähne putzen**	['tsɛ:nə 'putsən]
to shave (vi)	**sich rasieren**	[ziħ ra'zi:rən]
shaving foam	**Rasierschaum** (m)	[ra'zi:r'ʃaum]
razor	**Rasierer** (m)	[ra'zi:rə]
to wash (one's hands, etc.)	**waschen** (vt)	['va:ʃn]

to take a bath	sich waschen	[zɪḥ 'vaːʃn]
shower	Dusche (f)	['duʃə]
to take a shower	sich duschen	[zɪḥ 'duʃn]

bathtub	Badewanne (f)	['baːdə'vanə]
toilet (toilet bowl)	Klosettbecken (n)	[klɔ'zɛt'bɛkən]
sink (washbasin)	Waschbecken (n)	['vaːʃbəkn]

| soap | Seife (f) | ['zaɪfə] |
| soap dish | Seifenschale (f) | ['zaɪfən'ʃaːlə] |

sponge	Schwamm (m)	[ʃvam]
shampoo	Shampoo (n)	[ʃam'pɔː]
towel	Handtuch (n)	['hantʊh]
bathrobe	Bademantel (m)	['baːdə mantl]

laundry (process)	Wäsche (f)	['vɛʃə]
washing machine	Waschmaschine (f)	['vaʃma'ʃiːnə]
to do the laundry	waschen (vt)	['vaːʃn]
laundry detergent	Waschpulver (n)	['vaʃpʊlvə]

68. Household appliances

TV set	Fernseher (m)	['fɛrnzeːə]
tape recorder	Tonbandgerät (n)	['tonbandgə'rɛt]
video, VCR	Videorekorder (m)	['wiːdeɔ 'rekɔrdə]
radio	Empfänger (m)	[ɛmp'fɛŋə]
player (CD, MP3, etc.)	Player (m)	['plɛɪə]

video projector	Videoprojektor (m)	['wiːdeɔ prɔ'jektɔːr]
home movie theater	Heimkino (n)	['haɪm'kinɔ]
DVD player	DVD-Player (m)	[defau'deː 'plɛːɪə]
amplifier	Verstärker (m)	[fɛrʃ'tɛrkə]
video game console	Spielkonsole (f)	['ʃpiːlkɔnsɔlə]

video camera	Videokamera (f)	['wiːdeɔ 'kamərə]
camera (photo)	Kamera (f)	['kaːmərə]
digital camera	Digitalkamera (f)	[digi'tal 'kaːmərə]

vacuum cleaner	Staubsauger (m)	['ʃtaupzaugə]
iron (e.g., steam ~)	Bügeleisen (n)	['bygəlaɪzən]
ironing board	Bügelbrett (n)	['byːgəlb'rɛt]

telephone	Telefon (n)	['teːləfoːn]
mobile phone	Mobiltelefon (n)	[mɔ'biːl teləfoːn]
typewriter	Schreibmaschine (f)	['ʃraɪbmaʃiːnə]
sewing machine	Nähmaschine (f)	['nɛːmaʃiːnə]

| microphone | Mikrophon (n) | [mikrɔ'foːn] |
| headphones | Kopfhörer (m) | ['kɔpfhøːrə] |

remote control (TV)	**Fernbedienung** (f)	['fɛrnbə'diːnʊŋ]
CD, compact disc	**CD** (f)	[ʦeː'deː]
cassette	**Kassette** (f)	[ka'sɛtə]
vinyl record	**Schallplatte** (f)	['ʃalp'latə]

HUMAN ACTIVITIES

Job. Business. Part 1

69. Office. Working in the office

office (of firm)	**Büro** (n)	[by'rɔ:]
office (of director, etc.)	**Büro** (n)	[by'rɔ:]
front desk	**Rezeption** (f)	[reŀsɛp'ts'ɔ:n]
secretary	**Sekretär** (m)	[zekre'tɛ:r]
director	**Direktor** (m)	[di'rɛktɔ:r]
manager	**Manager** (m)	['mɛnədʒə]
accountant	**Buchhalter** (m)	['bʊhaltə]
employee	**Mitarbeiter** (m)	['mit 'arbaɪtə]
furniture	**Möbel** (n)	['mø:bl]
desk	**Tisch** (m)	[tiʃ]
desk chair	**Schreibtischstuhl** (m)	['ʃraptiʃtʊl]
chest of drawers	**Rollcontainer** (m)	['rɔlkɔn'tɛɪnə]
coat stand	**Kleiderständer** (m)	['klaɪdə 'ʃtɛndə]
computer	**Computer** (m)	[kɔm'pjy:tə]
printer	**Drucker** (m)	['drʊkə]
fax machine	**Fax** (n)	[faks]
photocopier	**Kopierer** (m)	[kɔ'pi:rə]
paper	**Papier** (n)	[pa'pi:ə]
office supplies	**Büromaterial** (n)	[by'rɔ matəri'al]
mouse pad	**Mousepad** (n)	['mauspet]
sheet (of paper)	**Bogen** (m)	['bɔ:gən]
folder, binder	**Mappe** (f)	['mapə]
catalog	**Katalog** (m)	[kata'lɔ:k]
phone book (directory)	**Adressbuch** (n)	[ad'rɛsbʊh]
documentation	**Dokumentation** (f)	[dɔkʊmɛnta'ts'ɔ:n]
brochure	**Broschüre** (f)	[brɔ'ʃyrə]
(e.g., 12 pages ~)		
leaflet	**Flugblatt** (n)	['flykblat]
sample	**Muster** (n)	['mʊstə]
training meeting	**Training** (n)	['trɛnin]
meeting (of managers)	**Beratung** (f)	['bəratʊn]
lunch time	**Mittagspause** (f)	['mita:ks 'pauzə]
to make a copy	**eine Kopie machen**	['aɪnə kɔ'pi: 'mahn]

to make copies	vervielfältigen (vt)	[fɛrˈfiːlˈfɛltigən]
to receive a fax	ein Fax bekommen	[aɪn faks ˈbəkɔmən]
to send a fax	ein Fax senden	[aɪn faks ˈsɛndən]

to call (by phone)	anrufen (vt)	[ˈanruːfən]
to answer (vt)	antworten (vi)	[ˈantvɔrtən]
to put through	verbinden (vt)	[fɛrˈbindən]

to arrange, to set up	ausmachen (vt)	[ˈausmahən]
to demonstrate (vt)	demonstrieren (vt)	[demɔnstˈriːrən]
to be absent	fehlen (vi)	[ˈfeːlən]
absence	Abwesenheit (f)	[apˈveːɛnhaɪt]

70. Business processes. Part 1

occupation	Beschäftigung (f)	[ˈbəʃɛftiguŋ]
firm	Firma (f)	[ˈfirma]
company	Gesellschaft (f)	[ˈgəzɛlʃaft]
corporation	Konzern (m)	[kɔnˈtsɛrn]
enterprise	Unternehmen (n)	[untərˈneːmən]
agency	Agentur (f)	[agɛnˈtuːr]

agreement (contract)	Vereinbarung (f)	[fɛˈraɪnbaruŋ]
contract	Vertrag (m)	[fɛrtˈraːk]
deal	Geschäft (n)	[ˈgəʃɛft]
order (to place an ~)	Auftrag (m)	[ˈauftraːk]
term (of contract)	Bedingung (f)	[ˈbədiŋuŋ]

wholesale (adv)	en gros	[ɛn ˈgrɔ]
wholesale (adj)	Großhandels-	[ˈgrɔːshandəls]
wholesale (n)	Großhandel (m)	[ˈgrɔːshandəl]
retail (adj)	Einzelhandels-	[ˈaɪntsəl ˈhandəl]
retail (n)	Einzelhandel (m)	[ˈaɪntsəl ˈhandəl]

competitor	Konkurrent (m)	[kɔŋkuˈrɛnt]
competition	Konkurrenz (f)	[kɔŋkuˈrɛnts]
to compete (vi)	konkurrieren (vi)	[kɔŋkuˈriːrən]

| partner (associate) | Partner (m) | [ˈpartnə] |
| partnership | Partnerschaft (f) | [ˈpartnəʃaft] |

crisis	Krise (f)	[ˈkriːzə]
bankruptcy	Bankrott (m)	[baŋkˈrɔːt]
to go bankrupt	Bankrott machen	[baŋkˈrɔːt ˈmahn]
difficulty	Schwierigkeit (f)	[ˈʃwiːriŋkaɪt]
problem	Problem (n)	[prɔbˈleːm]
catastrophe	Katastrophe (f)	[katastˈrɔːfə]

| economy | Wirtschaft (f) | [ˈwirtʃaft] |
| economic (~ growth) | wirtschaftlich | [ˈwirtʃaftliɲ] |

economic recession	**Rezession** (f)	[rɛtsɛ'sʲɔːn]
goal (aim)	**Ziel** (n)	[tsiːl]
task	**Aufgabe** (f)	['aufgaːbə]

to trade (vi)	**handeln** (vi)	['handəln]
network (distribution ~)	**Netz** (n)	[nɛts]
inventory (stock)	**Lager** (n)	['laːgə]
assortment	**Sortiment** (n)	[zɔrti'mɛnt]

leader (leading company)	**führende Unternehmen** (n)	['fyrəndə untər'neːmən]
large (~ company)	**groß**	[grɔːs]
monopoly	**Monopol** (n)	[mɔnɔ'pɔːl]

theory	**Theorie** (f)	[teɔ'riː]
practice	**Praxis** (f)	['praksis]
experience (in my ~)	**Erfahrung** (f)	[ɛr'faːrʊŋ]
trend (tendency)	**Tendenz** (f)	[tɛn'dɛnts]
development	**Entwicklung** (f)	[ɛnt'wiklʊŋ]

71. Business processes. Part 2

| benefit, profit | **Vorteil** (m) | [fɔːtaɪl] |
| profitable (adj) | **vorteilhaft** | ['fɔːrtaɪlhaft] |

delegation (group)	**Delegation** (f)	[delega'tsʲɔːn]
salary	**Lohn** (m)	[lɔːn]
to correct (an error)	**korrigieren** (vt)	[kɔri'giːrən]
business trip	**Dienstreise** (f)	['diːnst'raɪzə]
commission	**Kommission** (f)	[kɔmi'sʲɔːn]

to control (vt)	**kontrollieren** (vt)	[kɔntrɔ'liːrən]
conference	**Konferenz** (f)	[kɔnfe'rɛnts]
license	**Lizenz** (f)	[li'tsɛnts]
reliable (~ partner)	**zuverlässig**	['tsufɛrlɛsiɲ]

initiative (undertaking)	**Initiative** (f)	[initsia'tiːvə]
norm (standard)	**Norm** (f)	[nɔrm]
circumstance	**Umstand** (m)	['umʃtant]
duty (of employee)	**Pflicht** (f)	[pfliɲt]

organization (company)	**Unternehmen** (n)	[untər'neːmən]
organization (process)	**Organisation** (f)	[ɔrganiza'tsʲɔːn]
organized (adj)	**organisiert**	[ɔrgani'ziːrt]
cancellation	**Abschaffung** (f)	['apʃafʊŋ]
to cancel (call off)	**abschaffen** (vt)	['apʃafən]
report (official ~)	**Bericht** (m)	['bəriɲt]

| patent | **Patent** (n) | [pa'tɛnt] |
| to patent (obtain patent) | **patentieren** (vt) | [patɛn'tiːrən] |

to plan (vt)	planen (vt)	['pla:nən]
bonus (money)	Prämie (f)	['prɛmiə]
professional (adj)	professionell	[prɔfɛsɨɔ'nɛl]
procedure	Prozedur (f)	[prɔtse'du:r]

to examine (contract, etc.)	prüfen (vt)	['pry:fən]
calculation	Berechnung (f)	['bərɛhnʊŋ]
reputation	Ruf (m)	[rʊ:f]
risk	Risiko (n)	['ri:zikɔ]

to manage, to run	leiten (vt)	['laɪtən]
information	Information (f)	[ɪnfɔrma'tsɨɔnən]
property	Eigentum (n)	['aɪgəntʊm]
union	Bund (m)	[bʊnt]

life insurance	Lebensversicherung (f)	['le:bəns fɛr'zihərʊŋ]
to insure (vt)	versichern (vt)	[fɛr'zihərn]
insurance	Versicherung (f)	[fɛr'zihərʊŋ]

auction (~ sale)	Auktion (f)	[aʊk'tsɨɔ:n]
to notify (inform)	benachrichtigen (vt)	['bənahrihtigən]
management (process)	Verwaltung (f)	[fɛr'valtʊŋ]
service (~ industry)	Dienst (m)	['di:nst]

forum	Forum (n)	['fɔ:rʊm]
to function (vi)	funktionieren (vi)	[fʊŋktsɨo'ni:rən]
stage (phase)	Etappe (f)	[ɛ'tapə]
legal (~ services)	juristisch	[ju'ristiʃ]
lawyer (legal expert)	Jurist (m)	[ju'rist]

72. Production. Works

plant	Werk (n)	[vɛrk]
factory	Fabrik (f)	[fab'ri:k]
workshop	Werkstatt (f)	['vɛrkʃtat]
works, production site	Betrieb (m)	['bətri:p]

industry	Industrie (f)	[indʊst'ri:]
industrial (adj)	Industrie-	[indʊst'ri:]
heavy industry	Schwerindustrie (f)	[ʃwe:r indʊst'ri:]
light industry	Leichtindustrie (f)	['laɪht indʊst'ri:]

products	Produktion (f)	[prɔduk'tsɨɔ:n]
to produce (vt)	produzieren (vt)	[prɔdʊtsi:rən]
raw materials	Rohstoff (m)	['rɔ:ʃtɔf]

| foreman | Vorarbeiter (m), Meister (m) | [fɔ:rar'baɪtə, 'maɪstə] |

| workers team | Arbeitsteam (n) | ['arbaɪts'ti:m] |
| worker | Arbeiter (m) | ['arbaɪtə] |

working day	**Arbeitstag** (m)	['arbaɪtsta:k]
pause	**Pause** (f)	['pauzə]
meeting	**Versammlung** (f)	[fɛr'zamluŋ]
to discuss (vt)	**besprechen** (vt)	['bəʃprɛhn]

plan	**Plan** (m)	[pla:n]
to fulfill the plan	**den Plan erfüllen**	[den pla:n ɛr'fylən]
rate of output	**Leistungsnorm** (f)	['laɪstuŋsnɔ:rm]
quality	**Qualität** (f)	[kvali'tɛt]
checking (control)	**Prüfung, Kontrolle** (f)	['pry:fuŋ], [kɔnt'rɔlə]
quality control	**Gütekontrolle** (f)	['gytəkɔnt'rɔ:lə]

work safety	**Sicherheitstechnik** (f)	['zihərhaɪts 'tɛhnik]
discipline	**Disziplin** (f)	[distsip'li:n]
violation	**Übertretung** (f)	[ju:bət're:tuŋ]
(of safety rules, etc.)		
to violate (rules)	**übertreten** (vt)	['ju:bərtretən]

strike	**Streik** (m)	[ʃtraɪk]
striker	**Streikende** (m)	['ʃtraɪkəndə]
to be on strike	**streiken** (vi)	['ʃtraɪkən]
labor union	**Gewerkschaft** (f)	['gəvɛrkʃaft]

to invent (machine, etc.)	**erfinden** (vt)	[ɛr'findən]
invention	**Erfindung** (f)	[ɛr'finduŋ]
research	**Erforschung** (f)	[ɛr'fɔrʃuŋ]
to improve (make better)	**verbessern** (vt)	[fɛr'bɛsərn]
technology	**Technologie** (f)	[tɛhnɔlɔ'gi:]
technical drawing	**Zeichnung** (f)	['tsaɪhnuŋ]

load, cargo	**Ladung** (f)	['laduŋ]
loader (person)	**Ladearbeiter** (m)	['la:də'arbaɪtə]
to load (vehicle, etc.)	**laden** (vt)	['la:dən]
loading (process)	**Verladung** (f)	[fɛr'laduŋ]

| to unload (vi, vt) | **entladen** (vt) | [ɛnt'la:dən] |
| unloading | **Entladung** (f) | [ɛnt'la:duŋ] |

transportation	**Transport** (m)	[trans'pɔrt]
transportation company	**Transportunternehmen**	[trans'pɔrt untər'ne:mən]
to transport (vt)	**transportieren** (vt)	[transpɔr'ti:rən]

freight car	**Güterwagen** (m)	['gy:tə'va:gən]
cistern	**Zisterne** (f)	[tsis'tɛrnə]
truck	**Lastkraftwagen** (m)	['lastkraft 'va:gən]

| machine tool | **Werkzeugmaschine** (f) | ['vɛrktsɔɪk ma'ʃi:nə] |
| mechanism | **Mechanismus** (m) | [meha'nismus] |

industrial waste	**Industrieabfälle** (pl)	[indust'ri: 'apfələ]
packing (process)	**Einpacken** (n)	['aɪnpakən]
to pack (vt)	**verpacken** (vt)	[fɛr'pakən]

73. Contract. Agreement

contract	**Vertrag** (m)	[fɛrt'ra:k]
agreement	**Vereinbarung** (f)	[fɛ'raɪnbarʊŋ]
addendum	**Anhang** (m)	['anhaŋ]
to sign a contract	**einen Vertrag abschließen**	['aɪnən 'fɛrtrak apʃ'li:sən]
signature	**Unterschrift** (f)	['untərʃrift]
to sign (vt)	**unterschreiben** (vt)	[untərʃ'raɪbn]
stamp (seal)	**Stempel** (m)	['ʃtɛmpl]
subject of contract	**Vertragsgegenstand** (m)	[fɛrt'ra:ks 'ge:gənʃtant]
clause	**Punkt** (m)	[pʊŋkt]
parties (in contract)	**Parteien** (pl)	[par'taɪən]
legal address	**offizielle Adresse** (f)	[ɔfi'tsjele ad'rɛsə]
to break the contract	**Vertrag brechen**	[fɛrt'ra:k 'brɛhn]
commitment	**Verpflichtung** (f)	[fɛrp'liftʊŋ]
responsibility	**Verantwortlichkeit** (f)	[fɛrant'vɔrtlih kaɪt]
force majeure	**Force majeure** (f)	[fɔrs ma'ʒø:r]
dispute	**Streit** (m)	[ʃtraɪt]
penalties	**Strafsanktionen** (pl)	['ʃtra:f zaŋk'tsʲɔ:nən]

74. Import & Export

import	**Import** (m)	[im'pɔrt]
importer	**Importeur** (m)	[impɔr'tø:r]
to import (vt)	**importieren** (vt)	[impɔr'ti:rən]
import (e.g., ~ goods)	**Import-**	[im'pɔrt]
export	**Export** (m)	[ɛks'pɔrt]
exporter	**Exporteur** (m)	[ɛkspɔr'tø:r]
to export (vi, vt)	**exportieren** (vt)	[ɛkspɔr'ti:rən]
export (e.g., ~ goods)	**Export-**	[ɛks'pɔrt]
goods	**Waren** (pl)	['va:rən]
consignment, lot	**Partie** (f), **Ladung** (f)	[par'ti:], ['la:dʊŋ]
weight	**Gewicht** (n)	['gəwiht]
volume	**Volumen** (n)	[vɔ'ly:mən]
cubic meter	**Kubikmeter** (m)	[kʊ'bi:k 'me:tə]
manufacturer	**Hersteller** (m)	['he:rʃ'tɛlə]
transportation company	**Transportunternehmen**	[trans'pɔrt untər'ne:mən]
container	**Container** (m)	[kɔn'tɛɪnə]
border	**Grenze** (f)	['grɛntsə]
customs	**Zollamt** (n)	['tsɔl amt]

customs duty	Zoll (m)	[tsɔl]
customs officer	Zollbeamte (m)	['tsɔl 'bəamtə]
smuggling	Schmuggel (m)	['ʃmʊːgl]
contraband (goods)	Schmuggelware (f)	['ʃmʊgəlvaːrə]

75. Finances

stock (share)	Aktie (f)	['aktsiə]
bond (certificate)	Obligation (f)	[ɔbligaˈtsˈɔːn]
bill of exchange	Wechsel (m)	['vɛksl]

| stock exchange | Börse (f) | ['børzə] |
| stock price | Aktienkurs (m) | ['aktsiən 'kʊrs] |

| to go down | billiger werden | ['biligə 'weːrdən] |
| to go up | teuer werden | ['tɔiə 'weːrdən] |

| shareholding | Anteil (m) | ['antail] |
| controlling interest | Mehrheitspaket (n) | ['meːrhaits paˈkeːt] |

investment	Investitionen (pl)	[invɛstiˈtsˈɔːnən]
to invest (vt)	investieren (vt)	[invɛsˈtiːrən]
percent	Prozent (n)	[proˈtsɛnt]
interest (on investment)	Zinsen (pl)	['tsinzən]

profit	Gewinn (m)	['gəwin]
profitable (adj)	gewinnbringend	['gəwiːnbriːŋənt]
tax	Steuer (f)	['ʃtɔiə]

currency (foreign ~)	Währung (f)	['vɛrʊŋ]
national (adj)	Landes-	['landəs]
exchange (currency ~)	Geldumtausch (m)	['gɛldʊm'tauʃ]

| accountant | Buchhalter (m) | ['bʊhaltə] |
| accounting | Buchhaltung (f) | ['bʊˈhaltʊŋ] |

bankruptcy	Bankrott (m)	[baŋkˈrɔːt]
collapse, crash	Zusammenbruch (m)	[tsuˈzamənbrʊh]
ruin	Pleite (f)	['plaitə]
to be ruined	pleite gehen	['plaitə 'geːən]
inflation	Inflation (f)	[inflaˈtsˈɔːn]
devaluation	Abwertung (f)	['apvərtʊŋ]

capital	Kapital (n)	[kapiˈtaːl]
income	Einkommen (n)	['aiŋkɔmən]
turnover	Umsatz (m)	['umzats]
resources	Mittel (pl)	['mitl]
monetary resources	Geldmittel (n)	['gɛlt 'mitl]
overhead	Gemeinkosten (pl)	['gəmaiŋkɔstən]
to reduce (expenses)	reduzieren (vt)	[redʊˈtsiːrən]

76. Marketing

marketing	**Marketing** (n)	[mar'ketɪŋ]
market	**Markt** (m)	[markt]
market segment	**Marktsegment** (n)	['markt zeg'mɛnt]
product	**Produkt** (n)	[prɔ'dʊkt]
goods	**Waren** (pl)	['vaːrən]
trademark	**Handelsmarke** (f)	['handəls 'markə]
logotype	**Firmenzeichen** (n)	['firmən'tsaɪhn]
logo	**Logo** (n)	['lʊ.gɔ]
demand	**Nachfrage** (f)	['naːhfraːgə]
supply	**Angebot** (n)	['aŋ eːbɔt]
need	**Bedürfnis** (n)	['bədøːrfnis]
consumer	**Verbraucher** (m)	[fɛrb'rauhə]
analysis	**Analyse** (f)	[ana'lyːzə]
to analyze (vt)	**analysieren** (vt)	[analy'ziːrən]
positioning	**Positionierung** (f)	[pozi'tsʲɔ:'nirʊŋ]
to position (vt)	**positionieren** (vt)	[pozitsʲɔ'niːrən]
price	**Preis** (m)	[praɪs]
pricing policy	**Preispolitik** (f)	['praɪspolitik]
formation of price	**Preisbildung** (f)	['praɪsbildʊŋ]

77. Advertising

advertising	**Werbung** (f)	['vɛrbʊŋ]
to advertise (vt)	**werben** (vt)	['vɛrbn]
budget	**Budget** (n)	[by'dʒeː]
ad, advertisement	**Werbeanzeige** (f)	['vɛrbə 'antsaɪgə]
TV advertising	**Fernsehwerbung** (f)	['fɛrnzeːə 'vɛrbʊŋ]
radio advertising	**Radiowerbung** (f)	['radiɔ 'vɛrbʊŋ]
outdoor advertising	**Außenwerbung** (f)	['ausən 'vɛrbʊŋ]
mass media	**Massenmedien** (pl)	['masən 'meːdiən]
periodical (n)	**Zeitschrift** (f)	['tsaɪtʃrift]
image (public appearance)	**Image** (n)	['imidʒ]
slogan	**Losung** (f)	['loːzuŋ]
motto (maxim)	**Motto** (n)	['mɔtɔ]
campaign	**Kampagne** (f)	[kam'paɲə]
advertising campaign	**Werbekampagne** (f)	['vɛrbəkam'paɲə]
target group	**Zielgruppe** (f)	['tsiːlgrʊ:pə]
business card	**Visitenkarte** (f)	[wi'ziːtən 'kartə]
leaflet	**Flugblatt** (n)	['flykblat]

brochure (e.g., 12 pages ~)	**Broschüre** (f)	[brɔˈʃyrə]
pamphlet	**Faltblatt** (n)	[ˈfaltblat]
newsletter	**Informationsblatt** (n)	[informaˈtsʲɔ:ns bla:t]
store sign	**Ladenschild** (n)	[la:dənʃilt]
poster	**Plakat** (n)	[plaˈka:t]
billboard	**Werbeschild** (n)	[ˈvɛrbəʃilt]

78. Banking

bank	**Bank** (f)	[baŋk]
branch (of bank, etc.)	**Filiale** (f)	[filiˈa:lə]
bank clerk, consultant	**Berater** (m)	[ˈbəra:tə]
manager (director)	**Leiter** (m)	[ˈlaɪtə]
banking account	**Konto** (n)	[ˈkɔntɔ]
account number	**Kontonummer** (f)	[ˈkɔntɔˈnʊmə]
checking account	**Kontokorrent** (n)	[ˈkɔntɔkɔˈrɛnt]
savings account	**Sparkonto** (n)	[ˈʃpa:rkɔntɔ]
to open an account	**ein Konto eröffnen**	[aɪn ˈkɔntɔ ˈərøfnən]
to close the account	**das Konto schließen**	[das ˈkɔntɔ ˈʃli:sən]
to deposit into the account	**einzahlen** (vt)	[ˈaɪntsa:lən]
to withdraw (vt)	**abheben** (vt)	[ˈaphe:bn]
deposit	**Einzahlung** (f)	[ˈaɪntsa:lʊŋ]
to make a deposit	**eine Einzahlung machen**	[ˈaɪnə aɪnˈtsa:lʊŋ ˈmahn]
wire transfer	**Überweisung** (f)	[ju:bərˈvaɪzʊŋ]
to wire, to transfer	**überweisen** (vt)	[ju:bərˈvaɪzən]
sum	**Summe** (f)	[ˈzumə]
How much?	**Wieviel?**	[ˈwi:fi:l]
signature	**Unterschrift** (f)	[ˈuntərʃrift]
to sign (vt)	**unterschreiben** (vt)	[untərʃˈraɪbn]
credit card	**Kreditkarte** (f)	[kreˈdi:t ˈkartə]
code	**Code** (m)	[ˈkɔ:də]
credit card number	**Kreditkartennummer** (f)	[kreˈdi:t ˈkartə ˈnʊmə]
ATM	**Geldautomat** (m)	[ˈgɛlt aʊtɔˈma:t]
check	**Scheck** (m)	[ʃɛk]
to write a check	**einen Scheck schreiben**	[ˈaɪnən ʃɛk ˈʃraɪbn]
checkbook	**Scheckbuch** (n)	[ˈʃɛkbʊh]
loan (bank ~)	**Darlehen** (m)	[da:əˈle:ən]
to apply for a loan	**Darlehenantrag zu stellen**	[da:əˈle:ən ˈantra:k tsu ˈʃtɛlən]

to get a loan	ein Darlehen aufnehmen	[aɪn daːəˈleːən aʊfˈneːmən]
to give a loan	ein Darlehen geben	[aɪn daːəˈleːən geːbn]
guarantee	Pfand (n)	[pfant]

79. Telephone. Phone conversation

telephone	Telefon (n)	[ˈteːləfɔːn]
mobile phone	Mobiltelefon (n)	[mɔˈbiːl teləˈfɔːn]
answering machine	Anrufbeantworter (m)	[ˈanrʊːfbə ˈantvɔrtə]

| to call (telephone) | anrufen (vt) | [ˈanrʊ.fən] |
| phone call | Anruf (m) | [ˈanrʊːf] |

to dial a number	eine Nummer wählen	[ˈaɪnə ˈnʊmə ˈvɛlən]
Hello!	Hallo!	[haˈløː]
to ask (vt)	fragen (vt)	[ˈfraːgən]
to answer (vi, vt)	antworten (vi)	[ˈantvɔrtən]

to hear (vt)	hören (vt)	[ˈhøːrən]
well (adv)	gut	[gʊːt]
not well (adv)	schlecht	[ˈʃleħt]
noises (interference)	Störungen (pl)	[ˈʃtøːrʊŋən]

receiver	Hörer (m)	[ˈhøːrə]
to pick up (~ the phone)	den Hörer abnehmen	[den ˈhøːrə abˈneːmən]
to hang up (~ the phone)	auflegen (vt)	[ˈaʊfleːgən]

busy (adj)	besetzt	[ˈbəzɛtst]
to ring (ab. phone)	läuten (vi)	[ˈlɔɪtən]
telephone book	Telefonbuch (n)	[ˈteːləfɔːn bʊh]

local (adj)	Orts-	[ɔrts]
long distance (~ call)	interurban	[intərʊrˈban]
international (adj)	Auslands-	[ˈaʊslants]

80. Mobile telephone

mobile phone	Mobiltelefon (n)	[mɔˈbiːl teləˈfɔːn]
display	Display (n)	[dispˈlɛɪ]
button	Knopf (m)	[knɔpf]
SIM card	SIM-Karte (f)	[zim ˈkartə]

battery	Batterie (f)	[batəˈriː]
to be dead (battery)	leer sein	[ˈleːə zaɪn]
charger	Ladevorrichtung (f)	[ˈlaːdəfɔrˈrihtʊŋ]

| menu | Menü (n) | [meˈnyː] |
| settings | Einstellungen (pl) | [ˈaɪnʃtəlʊŋən] |

tune (melody)	Melodie (f)	[melɔ'diː]
to select (vt)	auswählen (vt)	['ausvɛlən]
calculator	Rechner (m)	['rɛhnə]
voice mail	Anrufbeantworter (m)	['anrɪ·fhə 'antvɔrtə]
alarm clock	Wecker (m)	['vɛkə]
contacts	Kontakte (pl)	[kɔn'taktə]
SMS (text message)	SMS-Nachricht (f)	[ɛse'mɛs 'naːhrɪft]
subscriber	Teilnehmer (m)	['taɪlneːmə]

81. Stationery

ballpoint pen	Kugelschreiber (m)	['kuːgl 'ʃraɪbə]
fountain pen	Federhalter (m)	['feːdər'haltə]
pencil	Bleistift (m)	['blaɪʃtift]
highlighter	Faserschreiber (m)	['fazərʃraɪbə]
felt-tip pen	Filzstift (m)	['filtsʃtift]
notepad	Notizblock (m)	[nɔ'tiːtsblɔk]
agenda (diary)	Terminkalender (m)	[ter'miːn ka'lɛndə]
ruler	Lineal (n)	[line'aːl]
calculator	Rechner (m)	['rɛhnə]
eraser	Radiergummi (m)	[ra'diːr'gumi]
thumbtack	Reißzwecke (f)	['raɪstsvəkə]
paper clip	Heftklammer (f)	['hɛftklamə]
glue	Klebstoff (m)	['klepʃtɔf]
stapler	Hefter (m)	['hɛftə]
hole punch	Locher (m)	['løhə]
pencil sharpener	Bleistiftspitzer (m)	['blaɪʃtift 'ʃpitsə]

82. Kinds of business

accounting services	Buchführung (f)	['buh'fyːruŋ]
advertising	Werbung (f)	['vɛrbuŋ]
advertising agency	Werbeagentur (f)	['vɛrbə agɛn'tuːr]
air-conditioners	Klimaanlagen (pl)	['kliːma 'anlaːgən]
airline	Fluggesellschaft (f)	['flykgəzɛlʃaft]
alcoholic drinks	Spirituosen (pl)	[ʃpiritu'ɔːzən]
antiquities	Antiquitäten (pl)	[antikwi'tɛtən]
art gallery	Kunstgalerie (f)	['kunstgale'riː]
audit services	Rechnungsprüfung (f)	['rɛhnuŋs 'pryːfun]
banks	Bankwesen (n)	['baŋkvəzən]
bar	Bar (f)	[baːr]

beauty parlor	Schönheitssalon (m)	[ˈʃønhaɪts zaˈlɔːn]
bookstore	Buchhandlung (f)	[ˈbʊhandluŋ]
brewery	Bierbrauerei (f)	[ˈbiːrbraʊəˈraɪ]
business center	Geschäftszentrum (n)	[ˈɡəʃɛftsɛntrʊm]
business school	Business-Schule (f)	[ˈbɪznəs ˈʃuːlə]

casino	Kasino (n)	[kaˈziːnɔ]
construction	Bau (m)	[ˈbau]
consulting	Beratung (f)	[ˈbəratʊŋ]

dental clinic	Stomatologie (f)	[stɔmatɔlɔˈgiː]
design	Design (n)	[dɪˈzaɪn]
drugstore, pharmacy	Apotheke (f)	[apɔˈteːkə]
dry cleaners	chemische Reinigung (f)	[ˈheːmiʃə ˈraɪnigʊŋ]
employment agency	Personalagentur (f)	[pɛrzɔˈnaːl agɛnˈtuːr]

financial services	Finanzdienstleistungen	[fiˈnants ˈdinstlaɪstʊŋən]
food products	Nahrungsmittel (pl)	[ˈnaːrʊŋsˈmitl]
funeral home	Bestattungsanstalt (f)	[ˈbəʃtatʊŋs ˈanʃtalt]
furniture (e.g., house ~)	Möbel (n)	[ˈmøːbl]
garment	Kleidung (f)	[ˈklaɪdʊŋ]
hotel	Hotel (n)	[hɔˈtɛl]

ice-cream	Eis (n)	[aɪs]
industry	Industrie (f)	[indʊstˈriː]
insurance	Versicherung (f)	[fɛrˈzihərʊŋ]
Internet	Internet (n)	[intərˈnɛt]
investment	Investitionen (pl)	[invɛstiˈtsɪɔːnən]

jeweler	Juwelier (m)	[juweˈliːr]
jewelry	Juwelierwaren (pl)	[juweˈliːrˈvaːrən]
laundry (shop)	Wäscherei (f)	[vɛʃəˈraɪ]
legal advisor	Rechtsberatung (f)	[ˈrɛhtsbeˈraːtʊŋ]
light industry	Leichtindustrie (f)	[ˈlaɪht indʊstˈriː]

magazine	Zeitschrift (f)	[ˈtsaɪtʃrift]
mail-order selling	Versandhandel (m)	[fɛrzantˈhandəl]
medicine	Medizin (f)	[mediˈtsiːn]
movie theater	Kino (n)	[ˈkiːnɔ]
museum	Museum (n)	[mʊˈzɛum]

news agency	Nachrichtenagentur (f)	[ˈnahrihtən agɛnˈtuːr]
newspaper	Zeitung (f)	[ˈtsaɪtʊŋ]
nightclub	Nachtklub (m)	[ˈnahtklup]

oil (petroleum)	Erdöl (n)	[ˈeːrt øːl]
parcels service	Kurierdienst (m)	[kʊrjeːˈdinst]
pharmaceuticals	Pharmaindustrie (f)	[ˈfarma indʊstˈriː]
printing (industry)	Polygraphie (f)	[pɔligraˈfiː]
publishing house	Verlag (m)	[fɛrˈlaːk]
radio (~ station)	Rundfunk (m)	[ˈrʊntfʊŋk]
real estate	Immobilien (pl)	[imɔˈbiːliən]

restaurant	**Restaurant** (n)	[rɛstoˈran]
security agency	**Sicherheitsagentur** (f)	[ˈzihərhaɪts aːgɛnˈtuːr]
sports	**Sport** (m)	[ʃpɔrt]
stock exchange	**Börse** (f)	[ˈbørzə]
store	**Laden** (m)	[ˈlaːdən]
supermarket	**Supermarkt** (m)	[ˈzupərmarkt]
swimming pool	**Schwimmbad** (n)	[ˈʃwimbat]
tailors	**Atelier** (n)	[ateˈʎje]
television	**Fernsehen** (n)	[ˈfɛrnzeːən]
theater	**Theater** (n)	[teˈaːtə]
trade	**Handel** (m)	[ˈhandəl]
transportation	**Transporte** (pl)	[transˈpɔrtə]
travel	**Reisen** (pl)	[ˈraɪzən]
veterinarian	**Tierarzt** (m)	[ˈtiːr ˈaːrtst]
warehouse	**Warenlager** (n)	[ˈvaːrən ˈlaːgə]
waste collection	**Müllabfuhr** (f)	[ˈmyˈlapfuːr]

Job. Business. Part 2

83. Show. Exhibition

exhibition, show	Ausstellung (f)	['ausʃtəluŋ]
trade show	Handelsausstellung (f)	['handəls 'ausʃtəluŋ]
participation	Teilnahme (f)	['taɪl'na:mə]
to participate (vi)	teilnehmen (vi)	['taɪlne:mən]
participant (exhibitor)	Teilnehmer (m)	['taɪlne:mə]
director	Direktor (m)	[di'rɛktɔ:r]
organizer's office	Organisationsbüro (n)	[ɔrganiza'tsʲɔ:ns by:'rɔ]
organizer	Organisator (m)	[ɔrgani'za:tɔ:r]
to organize (vt)	veranstalten (vt)	[fɛranʃ'taltən]
participation form	Anmeldeformular (n)	[an'mɛldə fɔmu'la:r]
to fill out (vt)	ausfüllen (vt)	['ausfylən]
details	Details (pl)	[de'taɪz]
information	Information (f)	[infɔrma'tsʲɔ:n]
price	Preis (m)	[praɪs]
including	einschließlich	['aɪnʃ'li:sliĥ]
to include (vt)	einschließen (vt)	['aɪnʃ'li:sən]
to pay (vi, vt)	zahlen (vt)	['tsa:lən]
registration fee	Anmeldegebühr (f)	['anməldəge'by:r]
entrance	Eingang (m)	['aɪŋ aŋ]
pavilion, hall	Pavillon (m)	[pawi'lɔn]
to register (vt)	registrieren (vt)	[regist'ri:rən]
badge (identity tag)	Namensschild (n)	['naməns ʃilt]
booth, stand	Stand (m)	[ʃtant]
to reserve, to book	reservieren (vt)	[rezər'wi:rən]
display case	Vitrine (f)	[wit'rinə]
spotlight	Strahler (m)	['ʃtralə]
design	Design (n)	[di'zaɪn]
to place (put, set)	stellen (vt)	['ʃtɛ:lən]
to be placed	gelegen sein	['gəle:gən zaɪn]
distributor	Distributor (m)	[distri'bʊ:tɔ:r]
supplier	Lieferant (m)	[li:fə'rant]
to supply (vt)	liefern (vt)	['li:fərn]
country	Land (n)	[lant]
foreign (adj)	ausländisch	['auslɛndiʃ]

product	**Produkt** (n)	[prɔ'dʊkt]
association	**Assoziation** (f)	[asɔtsia'tsʲɔːn]
conference hall	**Konferenzraum** (m)	[kɔnfə'rɛnts 'raum]
congress	**Kongress** (m)	[kɔŋ 'rɛs]
contest (competition)	**Wettbewerb** (m)	['vɛtbə'vɛrp]

visitor	**Besucher** (m)	['bəzuːhə]
to visit (attend)	**besuchen** (vt)	['bəzuːhən]
customer	**Auftraggeber** (m)	['auftraːk 'geːbə]

84. Science. Research. Scientists

science	**Wissenschaft** (f)	['wisənʃaft]
scientific (adj)	**wissenschaftlich**	['wisənʃaftliñ]
scientist	**Wissenschaftler** (m)	['wisənʃaftlə]
theory	**Theorie** (f)	[teɔ'riː]

axiom	**Axiom** (n)	[aksi'ɔm]
analysis	**Analyse** (f)	[ana'lyːzə]
to analyze (vt)	**analysieren** (vt)	[analy'ziːrən]
argument (strong ~)	**Argument** (n)	[argʊ'mɛnt]
substance (matter)	**Substanz** (f)	['zubstants]

hypothesis	**Hypothese** (f)	[hypɔ'tɛzə]
dilemma	**Dilemma** (n)	[di'lema]
dissertation	**Dissertation** (f)	[diserta'tsʲɔːn]
dogma	**Dogma** (n)	['dɔgma]

doctrine	**Doktrin** (f)	[dɔkt'riːn]
research	**Forschung** (f)	['fɔrʃʊŋ]
to do research	**forschen** (vi)	['fɔːrʃn]
testing	**Kontrolle** (f)	[kɔnt'rɔːlə]
laboratory	**Labor** (n)	[la'boːr]

method	**Methode** (f)	[me'toːdə]
molecule	**Molekül** (n)	[mɔle'kyːl]
monitoring	**Monitoring** (n)	[mɔni'tɔriŋ]
discovery (act, event)	**Entdeckung** (f)	[ɛnt'dɛkʊŋ]

postulate	**Postulat** (n)	[pɔstʊ'lat]
principle	**Prinzip** (n)	[prin'tsip]
forecast	**Prognose** (f)	[prɔg'nɔːzə]
prognosticate (vt)	**prognostizieren** (vt)	[prɔgnɔsti'tsiːrən]

synthesis	**Synthese** (f)	[zyn'tɛzə]
trend (tendency)	**Tendenz** (f)	[tɛn'dɛnts]
theorem	**Theorem** (n)	[teɔ'reːm]

| teachings | **Lehre** (f) | ['leːrə] |
| fact | **Tatsache** (f) | ['taːtzahə] |

| expedition | **Expedition** (f) | [ɛkspediˈtsɩɔːn] |
| experiment | **Experiment** (n) | [ɛkspɛriˈmɛnt] |

academician	**Akademiemitglied** (n)	[akadəˈmi mitglit]
bachelor (e.g., ~ of Arts)	**Bachelor** (m)	[ˈbɛtʃelə]
doctor (PhD)	**Doktor** (m)	[ˈdɔktɔːr]
Associate Professor	**Dozent** (m)	[dɔˈtsɛnt]
Master (e.g., ~ of Arts)	**Magister** (m)	[maˈgistə]
professor	**Professor** (m)	[prɔˈfɛsɔːr]

Professions and occupations

85. Job search. Dismissal

job	**Arbeit** (f), **Stelle** (f)	['arbaɪt], ['ʃtɛlə]
staff (work force)	**Belegschaft** (f)	['bəlekʃaft]
personnel	**Personal** (n)	[pɛrzɔ'naːʎ]
career	**Karriere** (f)	[ka'rjerə]
prospects	**Perspektive** (f)	[pɛrspɛk'tiːvə]
skills (mastery)	**Können** (n)	['kønən]
selection (screening)	**Auswahl** (f)	['ausvaːl]
employment agency	**Personalagentur** (f)	[pɛrzɔ'naːl agɛn'tuːr]
résumé	**Lebenslauf** (m)	['leːbəns'lauf]
interview (for job)	**Vorstellungsgespräch** (n)	['fɔːrʃ'tɛluŋs 'gəʃprɛh]
vacancy, opening	**Vakanz** (f)	[va'kants]
salary, pay	**Gehalt** (n)	['gəhalt]
fixed salary	**festes Gehalt** (n)	['fɛstəs 'gəhalt]
pay, compensation	**Arbeitslohn** (m)	['arbaɪts 'løːn]
position (job)	**Stellung** (f)	['ʃtɛluŋ]
duty (of employee)	**Pflicht** (f), **Aufgabe** (f)	[pfliht], [auf'gaːbə]
range of duties	**Aufgabenspektrum** (n)	['aufgabən 'ʃpɛktrʊm]
busy (I'm ~)	**beschäftigt**	['bəʃɛftiht]
to fire (dismiss)	**kündigen** (vt)	['kyndigən]
dismissal	**Kündigung** (f)	['kyndigʊŋ]
unemployment	**Arbeitslosigkeit** (f)	['arbaɪtslɔːzih kaɪt]
unemployed (n)	**Arbeitslose** (m)	['arbaɪtslɔːzə]
retirement	**Rente** (f), **Ruhestand** (m)	['rɛntə], ['ruːəʃtant]
to retire (from job)	**in Rente gehen**	[in 'rɛntə 'geːən]

86. Business people

director	**Direktor** (m)	[di'rɛktɔːr]
manager (director)	**Leiter** (m)	['laɪtə]
boss	**Boss** (m)	[bɔs]
superior	**Vorgesetzte** (m)	['fɔːrgə'zɛtstə]
superiors	**Vorgesetzten** (pl)	['fɔːrgə'zɛtstən]
president	**Präsident** (m)	[prɛzi'dɛnt]

chairman	Vorsitzende (m)	['fɔːrziːtsəndə]
deputy (substitute)	Stellvertreter (m)	['ʃtɛlfɛrtrɛtə]
assistant	Helfer (m)	['hɛlfə]
secretary	Sekretär (m)	[zekre'tɛːr]
personal assistant	Privatsekretär (m)	[pri'vaːt zekre'tɛːr]

businessman	Geschäftsmann (m)	['gəʃɛftsman]
entrepreneur	Unternehmer (m)	[untər'neːmə]
founder	Gründer (m)	['gryndə]
to found (vt)	gründen (vt)	['gryndən]

incorporator	Gründungsmitglied (n)	['gryndʊŋsmitklit]
partner	Partner (m)	['partnə]
stockholder	Aktionär (m)	[aktsio'nɛːr]

millionaire	Millionär (m)	[miʎo'nɛːr]
billionaire	Milliardär (m)	[miʎjar'dɛːr]
owner, proprietor	Besitzer (m)	['bezitsə]
landowner	Landbesitzer (m)	['lantbə'zitsə]

client	Kunde (m)	['kʊndə]
regular client	Stammkunde (m)	['ʃtamkʊndə]
buyer (customer)	Käufer (m)	['kɔɪfə]
visitor	Besucher (m)	['bəzuːhə]

professional (n)	Fachmann (m)	['fahman]
expert	Experte (m)	[ɛks'pɛrtə]
specialist	Spezialist (m)	[ʃpɛtsia'list]

| banker | Bankier (m) | [ba'ŋkiːə] |
| broker | Makler (m) | ['maklə] |

cashier, teller	Kassierer (m)	[ka'siːrə]
accountant	Buchhalter (m)	['bʊhaltə]
security guard	Wächter (m)	['vɛhtə]

investor	Investor (m)	[in'vɛstɔːr]
debtor	Schuldner (m)	['ʃʊldnə]
creditor	Gläubiger (m)	['glɔɪbigə]
borrower	Kreditnehmer (m)	[kre'diːt 'neːmə]

| importer | Importeur (m) | [impɔr'tøːr] |
| exporter | Exporteur (m) | [ɛkspɔr'tøːr] |

manufacturer	Hersteller (m)	['heːrʃtɛlə]
distributor	Distributor (m)	[distri'buːtɔːr]
middleman	Vermittler (m)	[fɛr'mitlə]

consultant	Berater (m)	['bəraːtə]
sales representative	Vertreter (m)	[fɛrt're:tə]
agent	Agent (m)	[agɛnt]
insurance agent	Versicherungsagent (m)	[fɛr'zihərʊŋs a'gɛnt]

87. Service professions

cook	**Koch** (m)	[kɔh]
chef (kitchen chef)	**Chefkoch** (m)	[ʃɛfkɔh]
baker	**Bäcker** (m)	['bɛkə]
bartender	**Barmixer** (m)	['baːrmiksə]
waiter	**Kellner** (m)	['kɛlnə]
waitress	**Kellnerin** (f)	['kɛlnərin]
lawyer, attorney	**Rechtsanwalt** (m)	['rɛhˈʦanvalt]
lawyer (legal expert)	**Jurist** (m)	[juˈrist]
notary	**Notar** (m)	[nɔˈtaːr]
electrician	**Elektriker** (m)	[ɛˈlektrikə]
plumber	**Klempner** (m)	['klempnə]
carpenter	**Zimmermann** (m)	['ʦimərman]
masseur	**Masseur** (m)	[maˈsøːr]
masseuse	**Masseurin** (f)	[maˈsøːrin]
doctor	**Arzt** (m)	[aːrʦt]
taxi driver	**Taxifahrer** (m)	['taksifaːrə]
driver	**Fahrer** (m)	['faːrə]
delivery man	**Ausfahrer** (m)	[aʊsˈfaːrə]
chambermaid	**Zimmermädchen** (n)	['ʦimərˈmɛːthən]
security guard	**Wächter** (m)	['vɛhtə]
flight attendant	**Flugbegleiterin** (f)	['flyk ˈbəglaɪtərin]
teacher (in primary school)	**Lehrer** (m)	['leːrə]
librarian	**Bibliothekar** (m)	[biblioˈteːkaːr]
translator	**Übersetzer** (m)	[juːbərˈzɛʦə]
interpreter	**Dolmetscher** (m)	['dɔlmətʃə]
guide	**Fremdenführer** (m)	['frɛmdən ˈfyːrə]
hairdresser	**Friseur** (m)	[friˈzøːr]
mailman	**Briefträger** (m)	['briːftrɛgə]
salesman (store staff)	**Verkäufer** (m)	[fɛrˈkɔɪfə]
gardener	**Gärtner** (m)	['gɛrtnə]
domestic servant	**Diener** (m)	['diːnə]
maid	**Magd** (f)	[makt]
cleaner (cleaning lady)	**Putzfrau** (f)	['pʊʦfrau]

88. Military professions and ranks

private	**Soldat** (m)	[zɔlˈdaːt]
sergeant	**Feldwebel** (m)	['feltweːbl]

| lieutenant | Leutnant (m) | ['løɪtnant] |
| captain | Hauptmann (m) | ['hauptman] |

major	Major (m)	[ma'joːr]
colonel	Oberst (m)	['ɔːbɐst]
general	General (m)	[genə'raːl]
marshal	Marschall (m)	['marʃaːl]
admiral	Admiral (m)	[admi'raːl]

military man	Militärperson (f)	[mili'tɛːr pɛr'zoːn]
soldier	Soldat (m)	[zɔl'daːt]
officer	Offizier (m)	[ɔfi'tsiːə]
commander	Kommandeur (m)	[kɔman'døːr]

border guard	Grenzsoldat (m)	['grɛntszɔlda:t]
radio operator	Funker (m)	['fuŋkə]
scout (searcher)	Aufklärer (m)	['aufk'lerə]
pioneer (sapper)	Pionier (m)	[pio'niːə]
marksman	Schütze (m)	['ʃytsə]
navigator	Steuermann (m)	['ʃtɔɪəman]

89. Officials. Priests

| king | König (m) | ['køːniɦ] |
| queen | Königin (f) | ['køːnigin] |

| prince | Prinz (m) | [prints] |
| princess | Prinzessin (f) | [prin'tsɛsin] |

| tsar, czar | Zar (m) | [tsaːr] |
| czarina | Zarin (f) | ['tsaːrin] |

president	Präsident (m)	[prɛzi'dɛnt]
Secretary (~ of State)	Minister (m)	[mi'nistə]
prime minister	Ministerpräsident (m)	[mi'nistə prɛzi'dɛnt]
senator	Senator (m)	[ze'naːtoːr]

diplomat	Diplomat (m)	[diplo'maːt]
consul	Konsul (m)	['kɔnzul]
ambassador	Botschafter (m)	['boːtʃaftə]
advisor (military ~)	Ratgeber (m)	['raːtge:bə]

official (civil servant)	Beamte (m)	['beːamtə]
prefect	Präfekt (m)	[prɛfəkt]
mayor	Bürgermeister (m)	['byrgərmaɪstə]

| judge | Richter (m) | ['riɦtə] |
| district attorney (prosecutor) | Staatsanwalt (m) | ['ʃtaːts anvalt] |

| missionary | Missionar (m) | [misio'naːr] |

monk	Mönch (m)	['mønh]
abbot	Abt (m)	[apt]
rabbi	Rabbiner (m)	[ra'bi:nə]

vizier	Wesir (m)	[we'zi:r]
shah	Schach (n)	[ʃah]
sheikh	Scheich (m)	[ʃaɪh]

90. Agricultural professions

beekeeper	Bienenzüchter (m)	['bi:nən'tsyhtə]
herder, shepherd	Hirt (m)	[hirt]
agronomist	Agronom (m)	[agrɔ'nɔ:m]
cattle breeder	Viehzüchter (m)	['fi:tsyhtə]
veterinarian	Tierarzt (m)	['ti:r 'a:rtst]

farmer	Farmer (m)	['farmə]
winemaker	Winzer (m)	['wintsə]
zoologist	Zoologe (m)	[tsɔ:'lo:gə]
cowboy	Cowboy (m)	['kaubɔɪ]

91. Art professions

actor	Schauspieler (m)	['ʃauʃpi:lə]
actress	Schauspielerin (f)	['ʃauʃpi:lərin]

singer (masc.)	Sänger (m)	['zɛŋə]
singer (fem.)	Sängerin (f)	['zɛŋərin]

dancer (masc.)	Tänzer (m)	['tɛntsə]
dancer (fem.)	Tänzerin (f)	['tɛntsərin]

performing artist (masc.)	Künstler (m)	['kynstlə]
performing artist (fem.)	Künstlerin (f)	['kynstlərin]

musician	Musiker (m)	['mu:zikə]
pianist	Pianist (m)	[pia'nist]
guitar player	Gitarrist (m)	[gita'rist]

conductor (orchestra ~)	Dirigent (m)	[diri'gent]
composer	Komponist (m)	[kɔmpɔ'nist]
impresario	Manager (m)	['mɛnədʒə]

movie director	Regisseur (m)	[reʒi'søːr]
producer	Produzent (m)	[prɔdu'tsɛnt]
scriptwriter	Drehbuchautor (m)	['dre:buh 'autɔ:r]
critic	Kritiker (m)	['kritikə]
writer	Schriftsteller (m)	['ʃriftʃtələ]

poet	Dichter (m)	['dɪħtə]
sculptor	Bildhauer (m)	['bilthauə]
artist (painter)	Maler (m)	['maːlə]

juggler	Jongleur (m)	[ʒɔŋ'løːr]
clown	Clown (m)	['klaun]
acrobat	Akrobat (m)	[akrɔ'baːt]
magician	Zauberkünstler (m)	['tsaubə'kynstlə]

92. Various professions

doctor	Arzt (m)	[aːrtst]
nurse	Krankenschwester (f)	['kraŋkən 'ʃvɛstə]
psychiatrist	Psychiater (m)	[psyhi'atə]
dentist	Zahnarzt (m)	[tsaːn 'aːrtst]
surgeon	Chirurg (m)	[hi'rʊrk]

astronaut	Astronaut (m)	[astrɔ'naut]
astronomer	Astronom (m)	[astrɔ'nɔːm]
pilot	Pilot (m)	[pi'lɔːt]

driver (of taxi, etc.)	Fahrer (m)	['faːrə]
engineer (train driver)	Lokomotivführer (m)	[lokɔmɔ'tiːf 'fyːrə]
mechanic	Mechaniker (m)	[me'haːnikə]

miner	Bergarbeiter (m)	['bɛrk 'arbaɪtə]
worker	Arbeiter (m)	['arbaɪtə]
metalworker	Schlosser (m)	['ʃlɔsə]
joiner (carpenter)	Tischler (m)	['tiʃlə]
turner	Dreher (m)	['dreːə]
construction worker	Bauarbeiter (m)	['bauarbaɪtə]
welder	Schweißer (m)	['ʃvaɪsə]

professor (title)	Professor (m)	[prɔ'fɛsɔːr]
architect	Architekt (m)	[arhi'tɛkt]
historian	Historiker (m)	[his'tɔːrikə]
scientist	Wissenschaftler (m)	['wisənʃaftlə]
physicist	Physiker (m)	['fyːzikə]
chemist (scientist)	Chemiker (m)	['heːmikə]

archeologist	Archäologe (m)	[arheɔ'lɔːgə]
geologist	Geologe (m)	[geɔ'lɔːgə]
researcher	Forscher (m)	['fɔrʃə]

| babysitter | Kinderfrau (f) | ['kində 'frau] |
| teacher, educator | Pädagoge (m) | [pɛda'gɔːgə] |

editor	Redakteur (m)	[redak'tøːr]
editor-in-chief	Chefredakteur (m)	['ʃɛf redak'tøːr]
correspondent	Korrespondent (m)	[kɔrɛspɔn'dɛnt]

typist (fem.)	Schreibkraft (f)	['ʃraɪpkraft]
designer	Designer (m)	[di'zaɪnɘ]
computer expert	Computerspezialist (m)	[kɔm'pjytɘ ʃpɘʦia'list]
programmer	Programmierer (m)	[prɔgra'miːrɘ]
engineer (designer)	Ingenieur (m)	[iŋʒɘ'nøːr]

sailor	Seemann (m)	['zeːman]
seaman	Matrose (m)	[mat'roːzɘ]
rescuer	Retter (m)	['rɛtɘ]

fireman	Feuerwehrmann (m)	['fɔɪɘ'weːr'man]
policeman	Polizist (m)	[poli'ʦist]
watchman	Nachtwächter (m)	[naht 'vɛhtɘ]
detective	Detektiv (m)	[detɛk'tiːf]

customs officer	Zollbeamte (m)	['ʦɔl 'bɘamtɘ]
bodyguard	Leibwächter (m)	['laɪpvɛhtɘ]
inspector	Inspektor (m)	[ins'pɛktɔːr]

sportsman	Sportler (m)	['ʃpɔrtlɘ]
trainer, coach	Trainer (m)	['trɛnɘ]
butcher	Fleischer (m)	['flaɪʃɘ]
cobbler	Schuster (m)	['ʃustɘ]
merchant	Geschäftsmann (m)	['gɘʃɛftsman]
loader (person)	Ladearbeiter (m)	['laːdɘ'arbaɪtɘ]

| fashion designer | Modeschöpfer (m) | [mɔːdɘ'ʃɛpfɘ] |
| model (fem.) | Modell (n) | [mɔ'dɛl] |

93. Occupations. Social status

| schoolboy | Schüler (m) | ['ʃyːlɘ] |
| student (college ~) | Student (m) | [ʃtʊ'dɛnt] |

philosopher	Philosoph (m)	[filo'zɔf]
economist	Ökonom (m)	[økɔ'noːm]
inventor	Erfinder (m)	[ɛr'findɘ]

unemployed (n)	Arbeitslose (m)	['arbaɪtslɔːzɘ]
retiree	Rentner (m)	['rɛntnɘ]
spy, secret agent	Spion (m)	[ʃpi'ɔːn]

prisoner	Gefangene (m)	['gɘfaŋɘnɘ]
striker	Streikende (m)	['ʃtraɪkɘndɘ]
bureaucrat	Bürokrat (m)	[byrok'rat]
traveler	Reisende (m)	['raɪzɘndɘ]

homosexual	Homosexuelle (m)	['hɔmɔzɛksʊ'ɛlɘ]
hacker	Hacker (m)	['hɛkɘ]
hippie	Hippie (m)	['hipi]

bandit	Bandit (m)	[ban'diːt]
hit man, killer	Killer (m)	['kilə]
drug addict	Drogenabhängiger (m)	['drɔːgən 'aphɛŋigə]
drug dealer	Drogenhändler (m)	['drɔgən 'hɛndlə]
prostitute (fem.)	Prostituierte (f)	[prɔstitu'iːrtə]
pimp	Zuhälter (m)	['tsuhɛltə]
sorcerer	Zauberer (m)	['tsaubərə]
sorceress	Zauberin (f)	['tsaubərin]
pirate	Seeräuber (m)	['zeːrɔɪbə]
slave	Sklave (m)	['sklaːvə]
samurai	Samurai (m)	[zamu'raɪ]
savage (primitive)	Wilde (m)	['wildə]

Education

94. School

school	**Schule** (f)	['ʃuːlə]
headmaster	**Schulleiter** (m)	['ʃuːlaɪtə]
pupil (boy)	**Schüler** (m)	['ʃyːlə]
pupil (girl)	**Schülerin** (f)	['ʃyːlərin]
schoolboy	**Schuljunge** (m)	[ʃuː'ljʊŋə]
schoolgirl	**Schulmädchen** (f)	[ʃuːl'mɛːthən]
to teach (sb)	**lehren** (vt)	['leːrən]
to learn (language, etc.)	**lernen** (vt)	['lɛrnən]
to learn by heart	**auswendig lernen**	['ausvɛndiɦ 'lernən]
to study (work to learn)	**lernen** (vi)	['lɛrnən]
to be in school	**in der Schule sein**	[in də 'ʃuːle zaɪn]
to go to school	**die Schule besuchen**	[di 'ʃuːle 'bəzuːhən]
alphabet	**Alphabet** (n)	[alfa'beːt]
subject (at school)	**Fach** (n)	[fah]
classroom	**Klasse** (f)	['klasə]
lesson	**Stunde** (f)	['ʃtʊndə]
recess	**Pause** (f)	['pauzə]
school bell	**Schulglocke** (f)	['ʃuːlgløkə]
school desk	**Schulbank** (f)	['ʃuːlbaŋk]
chalkboard	**Tafel** (f)	['taːfl]
grade	**Note** (f)	['nɔːtə]
good grade	**gute Note** (f)	['gʊːtə 'nɔːtə]
bad grade	**schlechte Note** (f)	['ʃlefɦtə 'nɔːtə]
to give a grade	**eine Note geben**	['aɪnə 'nɔːtə geːbn]
mistake, error	**Fehler** (m)	['fɛːlə]
to make mistakes	**Fehler machen**	['feːlə 'mahn]
to correct (an error)	**korrigieren** (vt)	[kɔri'giːrən]
cheat sheet	**Spickzettel** (m)	[ʃpik'ʦɛtl]
homework	**Hausaufgabe** (f)	['haus 'aufgaːbə]
exercise (in education)	**Übung** (f)	['juːbʊŋ]
to be present	**anwesend sein**	['anweːzənt zaɪn]
to be absent	**fehlen** (vi)	['feːlən]
to miss school	**versäumen** (vt)	[fɛr'zɔɪmən]

to punish (vt)	bestrafen (vt)	['bəʃtraːfən]
punishment	Strafe (f)	['ʃtraːfə]
conduct (behavior)	Benehmen (n)	['bəneːmən]

report card	Zeugnis (n)	['tsɔɪgnis]
pencil	Bleistift (m)	['blaɪʃtift]
eraser	Radiergummi (m)	[raˈdiːrˈgʊmi]
chalk	Kreide (f)	['kraɪdə]
pencil case	Federkasten (m)	['feːdərkastən]

schoolbag	Mappe (f)	['mapə]
pen	Kugelschreiber (m)	['kuːgl̩ˈʃraɪbə]
school notebook	Heft (n)	[hɛft]
textbook	Lehrbuch (n)	['leːrbʊh]
compasses	Zirkel (m)	['tsirkl̩]

to draw (a blueprint, etc.)	zeichnen (vt)	['tsaɪhnən]
technical drawing	Zeichnung (f)	['tsaɪhnʊŋ]

poem	Gedicht (n)	['gədiht]
by heart (adv)	auswendig	['ausvɛndih]
to learn by heart	auswendig lernen	['ausvɛndih 'lernən]

school vacation	Ferien (pl)	['feːriən]
to be on vacation	Ferien haben	['feːriən haːbn]
to spend one's vacation	Ferien verbringen	['feːriən fɛrbˈriŋən]

test (written math ~)	Test (m), Prüfung (f)	[tɛst], ['pryːfʊŋ]
essay (composition)	Aufsatz (m)	['aufzats]
dictation	Diktat (n)	[dikˈtaːt]
exam	Prüfung (f)	['pryːfʊŋ]
to take an exam	Prüfungen ablegen	['pryːfʊŋən 'apleːgən]
experiment (chemical ~)	Experiment (n)	[ɛkspɛriˈmɛnt]

95. College. University

academy	Akademie (f)	[akadəˈmiː]
university	Universität (f)	[univɛrziˈtɛːt]
faculty (section)	Fakultät (f)	[fakʊlˈtɛt]

student (masc.)	Student (m)	[ʃtʊˈdɛnt]
student (fem.)	Studentin (f)	[ʃtʊˈdɛntin]
lecturer (teacher)	Lehrer (m)	['leːrə]

lecture hall, room	Hörsaal (m)	[hørˈzaːl]
graduate	Hochschulabsolvent (m)	['hohʃʊːlapzɔlˈvɛnt]
diploma	Diplom (n)	[dipˈloːm]
dissertation	Dissertation (f)	[disertaˈtsˈɔːn]
study (report)	Forschung (f)	['forʃʊŋ]
laboratory	Labor (n)	[laˈbɔːr]

lecture	Lektion (f)	[lɛk'tsʲɔ:n]
course mate	Kommilitone (m)	[kɔmili'tɔ:nə]
scholarship	Stipendium (n)	[ʃti'pɛndium]
academic degree	akademischer Grad (m)	[aka'dɛ:miʃə gra:t]

96. Sciences. Disciplines

mathematics	Mathematik (f)	[matema'ti:k]
algebra	Algebra (f)	['algəbra]
geometry	Geometrie (f)	[geɔmet'ri:]
astronomy	Astronomie (f)	[astrɔnɔ'mi:]
biology	Biologie (f)	[biɔlɔ'gi:]
geography	Erdkunde (f)	['e:rtkʊndə]
geology	Geologie (f)	[geɔlɔ'gi:]
history	Geschichte (f)	['gəʃiħtə]
medicine	Medizin (f)	[medi'tsi:n]
pedagogy	Pädagogik (f)	[pɛda'gɔ:gik]
law	Recht (n)	[rɛħt]
physics	Physik (f)	[fy'zi:k]
chemistry	Chemie (f)	[he'mi:]
philosophy	Philosophie (f)	[filɔzɔ'fi:]
psychology	Psychologie (f)	[psyhɔlɔ'gi:]

97. Writing system. Orthography

grammar	Grammatik (f)	[gra'matik]
vocabulary	Lexik (f)	['lɛksik]
phonetics	Phonetik (f)	[fɔ:'ne:tik]
noun	Substantiv (n)	['zupstanti:f]
adjective	Adjektiv (n)	['adjekti:f]
verb	Verb (n)	[vɛrp]
adverb	Adverb (n)	[at'vɛrp]
pronoun	Pronomen (n)	[prɔ'nɔ:mən]
interjection	Interjektion (f)	[intərjek'tsʲɔ:n]
preposition	Präposition (f)	[prɛpɔzi'tsʲɔ:n]
root	Wurzel (f)	[vʊrtsl]
ending	Endung (f)	['ɛndʊŋ]
prefix	Vorsilbe (f)	['fɔ:rzilbə]
syllable	Silbe (f)	['zilbə]
suffix	Suffix (n), Nachsilbe (f)	[zu'fiks], ['na:hzilbə]
stress mark	Betonung (f)	['bətɔ:nʊŋ]

apostrophe	Apostroph (m)	[apɔst'rɔːf]
period, dot	Punkt (m)	[pʊŋkt]
comma	Komma (n)	['kɔːma]
semicolon	Semikolon (n)	[zemi'kɔːlɔn]

| colon | Doppelpunkt (m) | ['dɔpəlpʊŋkt] |
| ellipsis | Gedankenpunkte (pl) | ['gədaŋkən 'pʊŋktə] |

| question mark | Fragezeichen (n) | ['fraːgətsaɪhn] |
| exclamation point | Ausrufezeichen (n) | ['ausruː fə tsaɪhn] |

| quotation marks | Anführungszeichen (pl) | [anˈfyːrʊŋs ˈtsaɪhn] |
| in quotation marks | in Anführungszeichen | [in 'anfːjurʊŋs'tsaɪhn] |

| parenthesis | runde Klammern (pl) | ['rʊndə 'klamərn] |
| in parenthesis | in Klammern | [in 'klamərn] |

hyphen	Bindestrich (m)	['bindəʃtriħ]
dash	Gedankenstrich (m)	['gədaŋkən ʃtriħ]
space (between words)	Leerzeichen (n)	[leːə'tsaːɪhn]

| letter | Buchstabe (m) | ['bʊhʃtaːbə] |
| capital letter | Großbuchstabe (m) | ['grɔsbʊhʃtaːbə] |

| vowel (n) | Vokal (m) | [vɔ'kaːl] |
| consonant (n) | Konsonant (m) | [kɔnzɔ'nant] |

sentence	Satz (m)	[zaːts]
subject	Subjekt (n)	[zu'bjekt]
predicate	Prädikat (n)	[prɛdi'kaːt]

line	Zeile (f)	['tsaɪlə]
on a new line	in einer neuen Zeile	[in 'aɪnə 'nɔɪə 'tsaɪlə]
paragraph	Absatz (m)	['apzats]

word	Wort (n)	[vɔrt]
group of words	Wortverbindung (f)	['vɔrt fɛr'bindʊŋ]
expression	Redensart (f)	['reːdənzaːrt]

| synonym | Synonym (n) | [zynɔ'nyːm] |
| antonym | Antonym (n) | [antɔ'nym] |

rule	Regel (f)	['reːgl]
exception	Ausnahme (f)	['ausnaːmə]
correct (adj)	richtig	['riħtiħ]

conjugation	Konjugation (f)	[kɔnjuga'tsɔːn]
declension	Deklination (f)	[deklina'tsɔːn]
nominal case	Kasus (m)	['kaːzus]
question	Frage (f)	['fraːgə]
to underline (vt)	unterstreichen (vt)	[untərʃt'raɪhn]
dotted line	punktierte Linie (f)	[pʊŋk'tiːrtə 'liːniə]

98. Foreign languages

language	Sprache (f)	[ˈʃprahə]
foreign (adj)	Fremd-	[frɛmt]
to study (vt)	studieren (vt)	[ʃtuˈdiːrən]
to learn (language, etc.)	lernen (vt)	[ˈlɛrnən]

to read (vi, vt)	lesen (vi, vt)	[ˈleːzn]
to speak (vi, vt)	sprechen (vi, vt)	[ˈʃprɛhn]
to understand (vt)	verstehen (vt)	[fɛrʃˈteːən]
to write (vt)	schreiben (vi, vt)	[ʃraɪbn]

fast (adv)	schnell	[ʃnɛl]
slowly (adv)	langsam	[ˈlaŋzaːm]
fluently (adv)	fließend	[ˈfliːsənt]

rules	Regeln (pl)	[ˈreːgəln]
grammar	Grammatik (f)	[graˈmatik]
vocabulary	Vokabular (n)	[vɔkabuˈlaːr]
phonetics	Phonetik (f)	[fɔːˈneːtik]

textbook	Lehrbuch (n)	[ˈleːrbuh]
dictionary	Wörterbuch (n)	[ˈwørtəbuːh]
teach-yourself book	Selbstlernbuch (n)	[ˈzɛlpstˈlern buh]
phrasebook	Sprachführer (m)	[ˈʃprahfyːrə]
cassette	Kassette (f)	[kaˈsɛtə]
videotape	Videokassette (f)	[ˈwiːdeo kaˈsɛtə]
CD, compact disc	CD (f)	[tseːˈdeː]
DVD	DVD (f)	[defauˈdeː]

alphabet	Alphabet (n)	[alfaˈbeːt]
to spell (vt)	buchstabieren (vt)	[buhʃtaˈbiːrən]
pronunciation	Aussprache (f)	[ˈausʃprahə]

accent	Akzent (m)	[akˈtsɛnt]
with an accent	mit Akzent	[mit Akzent]
without an accent	ohne Akzent	[ˈɔnə akˈtsɛnt]

| word | Wort (n) | [vɔrt] |
| meaning | Bedeutung (f) | [ˈbədɔɪtuŋ] |

course (e.g., a French ~)	Kurse (pl)	[ˈkurzə]
to sign up	sich einschreiben	[ziñ ˈaɪnʃraɪbn]
teacher	Lehrer (m)	[ˈleːrə]

translation (process)	Übertragung (f)	[juːbertˈraguŋ]
translation (text, etc.)	Übersetzung (f)	[juːbərˈzɛtsun]
translator	Übersetzer (m)	[juːbərˈzɛtsə]
interpreter	Dolmetscher (m)	[ˈdɔlmətʃə]
polyglot	Polyglott (m, f)	[pɔlygˈlɔːt]
memory	Gedächtnis (n)	[ˈgədɛhtnis]

Rest. Entertainment. Travel

99. Trip. Travel

tourism	Tourismus (m)	[tʊːˈrismʊs]
tourist	Tourist (m)	[tɪˈriːt]
trip, voyage	Reise (f)	[ˈraɪzə]
adventure	Abenteuer (n)	[ˈabəntɔɪə]
trip, journey	Fahrt (f)	[faːrt]
vacation	Urlaub (m)	[ˈurlaup]
to be on vacation	auf Urlaub sein	[aʊf ˈuːrlaup zaɪn]
rest	Erholung (f)	[ɛrˈhɔːluŋ]
train	Zug (m)	[ʦuk]
by train	mit dem Zug	[mit dem ʦuk]
airplane	Flugzeug (n)	[ˈflykʦɔɪk]
by airplane	mit dem Flugzeug	[mit dem ˈflykʦɔɪk]
by car	mit dem Auto	[mit dem ˈautɔ]
by ship	mit dem Schiff	[mit dem ʃif]
luggage	Gepäck (n)	[ˈɡəpɛk]
suitcase, luggage	Koffer (m)	[ˈkɔfə]
luggage cart	Gepäckwagen (m)	[ˈɡəpɛkvaːgən]
passport	Pass (m)	[pas]
visa	Visum (n)	[ˈwiːzum]
ticket	Fahrkarte (f)	[ˈfaːrkartə]
air ticket	Flugticket (n)	[ˈflyk ˈtikət]
guidebook	Reisehandbuch (n)	[ˈraɪzə ˈhantbʊh]
map	Landkarte (f)	[ˈlantkartə]
area (rural ~)	Gegend (f)	[ˈgeːgənt]
place, site	Ort (m)	[ɔːrt]
exotic (n)	Exotik (f)	[ɛkˈzɔːtik]
exotic (adj)	exotisch	[ɛkˈzɔːtiʃ]
amazing (adj)	erstaunlich	[ɛrʃˈtaunliħ]
group	Gruppe (f)	[ˈgrʊpə]
excursion	Ausflug (m)	[ˈausfluːk]
guide (person)	Reiseleiter (m)	[ˈraɪzəlaɪtə]

100. Hotel

hotel	**Hotel** (n)	[hɔ'tɛl]
motel	**Motel** (n)	[mo'tɛl]
three-star	**drei Sterne**	['draɪ 'ʃtɛrnə]
five-star	**fünf Sterne**	['fynf 'ʃtɛrnə]
to stay (in hotel, etc.)	**absteigen** (vi)	['apʃtaɪgən]
room	**Hotelzimmer** (n)	[hɔ'tɛl 'tsimə]
single room	**Einzelzimmer** (n)	['aɪntsəl 'tsimə]
double room	**Zweibettzimmer** (n)	['tsvaɪbə 'tsimə]
to book a room	**reservieren** (vt)	[rezər'wiːrən]
half board	**Halbpension** (f)	['halpan'zʲɔːn]
full board	**Vollpension** (f)	['fɔlpan'zʲɔːn]
with bath	**mit Bad**	[mit 'baːt]
with shower	**mit Dusche**	[mit 'duʃə]
satellite television	**Satellitenfernsehen** (n)	[zatə'liːtən 'fɛrnzeːən]
air-conditioner	**Klimaanlage** (f)	['klima 'anlaːgə]
towel	**Handtuch** (n)	['hantʊh]
key	**Schlüssel** (m)	['ʃlysl]
administrator	**Verwalter** (m)	[fɛr'valtə]
chambermaid	**Zimmermädchen** (n)	['tsimər'mɛːthən]
porter, bellboy	**Träger** (m)	['trɛgə]
doorman	**Portier** (m)	[pɔr'tʲe]
restaurant	**Restaurant** (n)	[rɛstɔ'ran]
pub, bar	**Bar** (f)	[baːr]
breakfast	**Frühstück** (n)	['fryːʃtyk]
dinner	**Abendessen** (n)	['aːbnt 'ɛsən]
buffet	**Buffet** (n)	[by'feː]
lobby	**Foyer** (n)	[fɔa'jeː]
elevator	**Aufzug** (m), **Fahrstuhl** (m)	['auftsuk], ['faːrʃtʊːl]
DO NOT DISTURB	**BITTE NICHT STÖREN!**	['bitə niht 'ʃtøːrən]
NO SMOKING	**RAUCHEN VERBOTEN!**	['rauhən fɛr'bɔːtən]

TECHNICAL EQUIPMENT. TRANSPORTATION

Technical equipment

101. Computer

computer	Computer (m)	[kɔm'pjyːtə]
notebook, laptop	Laptop (m), Notebook (n)	['lɛptɔp], ['nɔutbʊk]
to turn on	einschalten (vt)	['aɪnʃaltən]
to turn off	abstellen (vt)	['apʃtɛlən]
keyboard	Tastatur (f)	[tasta'tuːr]
key	Taste (f)	['tastə]
mouse	Maus (f)	['maus]
mouse pad	Mousepad (n)	['mauspət]
button	Knopf (m)	[knɔpf]
cursor	Cursor (m)	['kørzə]
monitor	Monitor (m)	['mɔːnitɔːr]
screen	Schirm (m)	[ʃirm]
hard disk	Festplatte (f)	['fɛstplatə]
hard disk volume	Festplattengröße (f)	['fɛstplatən røsə]
memory	Speicher (m)	['ʃpaɪhə]
random access memory	Arbeitsspeicher (m)	['arbaɪtʃ'paɪhə]
file	Datei (f)	[da'taɪ]
folder	Ordner (m)	['ɔrdnə]
to open (vt)	öffnen (vt)	[øfnən]
to close (vt)	schließen (vt)	['ʃliːsən]
to save (vt)	speichern (vt)	['ʃpaɪhərn]
to delete (vt)	löschen (vt)	['løʃn]
to copy (vt)	kopieren (vt)	[kɔ'piːrən]
to sort (vt)	sortieren (vt)	[zɔr'tiːrən]
to transfer (copy)	transferieren (vt)	[transfe'rirən]
program	Programm (n)	[prɔg'ram]
software	Software (f)	[sɔft'vɛa]
programmer	Programmierer (m)	[prɔgra'miːrə]
to program (vt)	programmieren (vt)	[prɔgra'miːrən]
hacker	Hacker (m)	['hɛkə]
password	Kennwort (n)	['kɛnvɔrt]

| virus | **Virus** (n) | ['wi:rʊs] |
| to find, to detect | **entdecken** (vt) | [ɛnt'dɛkən] |

| byte | **Byte** (n) | [baɪt] |
| megabyte | **Megabyte** (n) | ['me:gabaɪt] |

| data | **Daten** (pl) | ['da:tən] |
| database | **Datenbank** (f) | ['datənbaŋk] |

cable (USB, etc.)	**Kabel** (n)	['ka:bl]
to disconnect (vt)	**abschalten** (vt)	['apʃaltən]
to connect (sth to sth)	**anschließen** (vt)	['anʃli:sən]

102. Internet. E-mail

Internet	**Internet** (n)	[intər'nɛt]
browser	**Browser** (m)	['brauzə]
search engine	**Suchmaschine** (f)	['zuhma'ʃi:nə]
provider	**Provider** (m)	[prɔ'vaɪdə]

web master	**Webmaster** (m)	['vɛp'mastə]
website	**Website** (f)	['vɛpsaɪt]
web page	**Webseite** (f)	['vɛp'tsaɪtə]

| address | **Adresse** (f) | [ad'rɛsə] |
| address book | **Adressbuch** (n) | [ad'rɛsbʊh] |

mailbox	**Mailbox** (f)	['mɛilbɔks]
mail	**Post** (f)	[pɔst]
full (adj)	**überfüllt**	[ju:bər'fylt]

message	**Mitteilung** (f)	['mitaɪluŋ]
incoming messages	**eingehenden Nachrichten** (pl)	[aɪn 'e:əndən 'nahrihtən]
outgoing messages	**ausgehenden Nachrichten**	['ausge:əndən 'na:hriħtən]

sender	**Absender** (m)	['apzəndə]
to send (vt)	**senden** (vt)	['zɛndən]
sending (of mail)	**Absendung** (f)	['apzənduŋ]

| receiver | **Empfänger** (m) | [ɛmp'fɛŋə] |
| to receive (vt) | **empfangen** (vt) | [ɛmp'fa:ŋən] |

| correspondence | **Briefwechsel** (m) | ['bri:fvəksl] |
| to correspond (vi) | **im Briefwechsel stehen** | [im 'brifvɛksəl 'ʃte:ən] |

file	**Datei** (f)	[da'taɪ]
to download (vt)	**herunterladen** (vt)	[hɛ'rʊntər'la:dən]
to create (vt)	**schaffen** (vt)	['ʃafən]

| to delete (vt) | löschen (vt) | ['løʃn] |
| deleted (adj) | gelöscht | [ge'løʃt] |

connection (ADSL, etc.)	Verbindung (f)	[fɛr'bindʊn]
speed	Geschwindigkeit (f)	['gəʃwindiħkaıt]
modem	Modem (n)	['mɔ:dəm]
access	Zugang (m)	['tsu:gan]
port (e.g., input ~)	Port (m)	[pɔrt]

| connection (make a ~) | Anschluss (m) | ['anʃlys] |
| to connect to ... (vi) | sich anschließen | [ziħ 'anʃli:sən] |

| to select (vt) | auswählen (vt) | ['ausvɛlən] |
| to search (for ...) | suchen (vt) | ['zu:hən] |

103. Electricity

electricity	Elektrizität (f)	[ɛlektritsi'tɛt]
electrical (adj)	elektrisch	[ɛ'lektriʃ]
electric power station	Elektrizitätswerk (n)	[ɛlektritsi'tɛtsvərk]
energy	Energie (f)	[ɛnər'gi:]
electric power	Strom (m)	[ʃtrɔ:m]

light bulb	Glühbirne (f)	['gly:birnə]
flashlight	Taschenlampe (f)	['taʃən'lampə]
street light	Straßenlaterne (f)	['ʃtrasən la'tɛrnə]

light	Licht (n)	[liħt]
to turn on	einschalten (vt)	['aınʃaltən]
to turn off	ausschalten (vt)	['ausʃaltən]
to turn off the light	das Licht ausschalten	[das liħt 'ausʃaltən]

to burn out (vi)	durchbrennen (vi)	['dʊrhb'rɛnən]
short circuit	Kurzschluss (m)	['kʊrtsʃlus]
broken wire	Riß (m)	[ris]
contact	Kontakt (m)	[kɔn'takt]

light switch	Schalter (m)	['ʃaltə]
wall socket	Steckdose (f)	['ʃtɛkdɔ:zə]
plug	Stecker (m)	['ʃtɛkə]
extension cord	Verlängerung (f)	[fɛr'lɛŋərʊn]

fuse	Sicherung (f)	['ziherʊn]
cable, wire	Draht (m)	[dra:t]
wiring	Verdrahtung (f)	[fɛrd'ra:tʊn]

ampere	Ampere (n)	[am'pɛ:r]
amperage	Stromstärke (f)	['ʃtrɔ:mʃtɛrkə]
volt	Volt (n)	[vɔlt]
voltage	Voltspannung (f)	['vɔlt 'ʃpanʊn]

| electrical device | Elektrogerät (n) | [ɛ'lektrɔgə'rɛt] |
| indicator | Indikator (m) | [indi'ka:tɔ:r] |

electrician	Elektriker (m)	[ɛ'lektrikə]
to solder (vt)	löten (vt)	['lø:tən]
soldering iron	Lötkolben (m)	['lø:tkɔlbən]
electric current	Strom (m)	[ʃtrɔ:m]

104. Tools

tool, instrument	Werkzeug (n)	['vɛrktsɔɪk]
tools	Werkzeuge (pl)	['vɛrktsɔɪgə]
equipment (factory ~)	Einrichtung (f)	['aɪnriʰtʊŋ]

hammer	Hammer (m)	['hamə]
screwdriver	Schraubenzieher (m)	['ʃraubəntsi:ə]
ax	Axt (f)	[akst]

saw	Säge (f)	['zɛgə]
to saw (vt)	sägen (vt)	['zɛgən]
plane (tool)	Hobel (m)	['hɔ:bl]
to plane (vt)	hobeln (vt)	['hɔ:bəln]
soldering iron	Lötkolben (m)	['lø:tkɔlbən]
to solder (vt)	löten (vt)	['lø:tən]

file (for metal)	Feile (f)	['faɪlə]
carpenter pincers	Kneifzange (f)	[knaɪfʦaŋə]
lineman's pliers	Flachzange (f)	['flahʦaŋə]
chisel	Stemmeisen (n)	[ʃtɛm 'aɪzən]

drill bit	Bohrer (m)	['bɔ:rə]
electric drill	Bohrmaschine (f)	[bɔ:rma'çinə]
to drill (vi, vt)	bohren (vt)	['bɔ:rən]

knife	Messer (n)	['mɛsə]
pocket knife	Taschenmesser (n)	['taʃən'mɛsə]
folding (~ knife)	Klapp-	[klap]
blade	Klinge (f)	['kliŋə]

sharp (blade, etc.)	scharf	[ʃarf]
blunt (adj)	stumpf	[ʃtʊmpf]
to become blunt	stumpf werden (vi)	[ʃtʊmpf 'we:rdən]
to sharpen (vt)	schärfen (vt)	['ʃɛrfən]

bolt	Bolzen (m)	['bɔltsən]
nut	Mutter (f)	['mʊtə]
thread (of a screw)	Gewinde (n)	['gəwində]
wood screw	Holzschraube (f)	['ʃraubə]
nail	Nagel (m)	['na:gəl]
nailhead	Nagelkopf (m)	['na:gəl kɔpf]

ruler (for measuring)	Lineal (n)	[line'a:l]
tape measure	Metermaß (n)	['me:tərmas]
spirit level	Wasserwaage (f)	['vasəva:gə]
magnifying glass	Lupe (f)	['lu:pə]

measuring instrument	Messinstrument (n)	[mɛsinstrʊ'mɛnt]
to measure (vt)	messen (vt)	['mɛsn]
scale	Skala (f)	['ska:la]
(of thermometer, etc.)		
readings	Ablesung (f)	[ap'lezuŋ]

| compressor | Kompressor (m) | [kɔmp'rɛsɔ:r] |
| microscope | Mikroskop (n) | [mikrɔs'kɔp] |

pump (e.g., water ~)	Pumpe (f)	['pʊmpə]
robot	Roboter (m)	['rɔbɔtə]
laser	Laser (m)	['le:zə]

wrench	Schraubenschlüssel (m)	['ʃraubən 'ʃlysl]
adhesive tape	Klebeband (n)	['kle:bəbant]
glue	Klebstoff (m)	['klepʃtɔf]

emery paper	Sandpapier (n)	['zantpa'pi:ə]
spring	Sprungfeder (f)	['ʃprʊŋfe:də]
magnet	Magnet (m)	[mag'ne:t]
gloves	Handschuhe (pl)	['hantʃu:ə]

rope	Leine (f)	['lainə]
cord	Schnur (f)	[ʃnʊr]
wire (e.g., telephone ~)	Draht (m)	[dra:t]
cable	Kabel (n)	['ka:bl]

sledgehammer	schwerer Hammer (m)	['ʃwe:rə 'hamə]
crowbar	Brecheisen (n)	['brɛhʲaɪzən]
ladder	Leiter (f)	['laitə]
stepladder	Trittleiter (f)	['tritlaitə]

to screw (tighten)	zudrehen (vt)	['tsudre:ən]
to unscrew, untwist (vt)	abdrehen (vt)	['apd're:ən]
to tighten (vt)	zusammendrücken (vt)	[tsu'zamən 'drykən]
to glue, to stick	ankleben (vt)	[aŋk'lebn]
to cut (vt)	schneiden (vt)	['ʃnaidən]

malfunction (fault)	Störung (f)	['ʃtø:rʊŋ]
repair (mending)	Reparatur (f)	[repara'tʊ:r]
to repair, to mend (vt)	reparieren (vt)	[repa'ri:rən]
to adjust (machine, etc.)	einstellen (vt)	['ainʃtələn]

to check (to examine)	prüfen (vt)	['pry:fən]
checking	Prüfung (f)	['pry:fʊŋ]
readings	Ablesung (f)	[ap'lezuŋ]
reliable (machine)	sicher	['zihə]

complicated (adj)	**kompliziert**	[kɔmpli'tsiːrt]
to rust (get rusted)	**verrosten** (vi)	[fɛ'rɔstən]
rusty, rusted (adj)	**rostig**	['rɔstiɦ]
rust	**Rost** (m)	[rɔst]

Transportation

105. Airplane

airplane	Flugzeug (n)	['flyktsɔʏk]
air ticket	Flugticket (n)	['flyk 'tikət]
airline	Fluggesellschaft (f)	['flykgəzɛlʃaft]
airport	Flughafen (m)	['flykha:fən]
supersonic (adj)	Überschall-	['ju:bərʃal]
captain	Flugkapitän (m)	['flyk kapitɛ:n]
crew	Besatzung (f)	['bəzatsuŋ]
pilot	Pilot (m)	[pi'lo:t]
flight attendant	Flugbegleiterin (f)	['flyk 'bəglaɪtərin]
navigator	Steuermann (m)	['ʃtɔɪəman]
wings	Flügel (pl)	['fly:gl]
tail	Schwanz (m)	[ʃvants]
cockpit	Kabine (f)	[ka'bi:nə]
engine	Motor (m)	['mo:tɔ:r]
undercarriage	Fahrgestell (n)	['fa:rgəʃ'tɛl]
turbine	Turbine (f)	[tʊr'bi:nə]
propeller	Propeller (m)	[prɔ'pɛlə]
black box	Flugschreiber (m)	['flykʃraɪbə]
control column	Steuerrad (n)	['ʃtɔɪəra:t]
fuel	Treibstoff (m)	['traɪpʃtɔf]
safety card	Sicherheitskarte (f)	['zihəhaɪts 'ka:rtə]
oxygen mask	Sauerstoffmaske (f)	['zauərʃtɔf 'maskə]
uniform	Uniform (f)	['unifɔrm]
life vest	Rettungsweste (f)	['rɛtʊŋs 'vɛ:stə]
parachute	Fallschirm (m)	['falʃirm]
takeoff	Abflug, Start (m)	['apflyk], [ʃtart]
to take off (vi)	aufsteigen, starten (vi)	[aʊf'taɪgən], ['ʃtartən]
runway	Startbahn (f)	['ʃtartba:n]
visibility	Sicht (f)	[ziht]
flight (act of flying)	Flug (m)	[flyk]
altitude	Höhe (f)	['hø:ə]
air pocket	Luftloch (n)	['lyft 'lɔh]
seat	Platz (m)	[plats]
headphones	Kopfhörer (m)	['kɔpfhø:rə]
folding tray	Klapptisch (m)	['klapti:ʃ]

| airplane window | **Bullauge** (n) | ['bʊ'laugə] |
| aisle | **Durchgang** (m) | ['dʊrɦgaŋ] |

106. Train

train	**Zug** (m)	[ʦuk]
suburban train	**elektrischer Zug** (m)	[ɛ'lektriʃə 'ʦuk]
express train	**Schnellzug** (m)	['ʃnɛlʦuk]
diesel locomotive	**Diesellok** (f)	['di:zə'lɔk]
steam engine	**Dampflok** (f)	['dampflɔk]
passenger car	**Eisenbahnwagen** (m)	['aɪzənba:n 'va:gən]
dining car	**Speisewagen** (m)	['ʃpaɪzəva:gən]
rails	**Schienen** (pl)	['ʃi:nən]
railroad	**Eisenbahn** (f)	['aɪzənba:n]
railway tie	**Bahnschwelle** (f)	['ba:nʃwelə]
platform (railway ~)	**Bahnsteig** (m)	['ba:nʃtaɪk]
track (~ 1, 2, etc.)	**Gleis** (n)	['glaɪs]
semaphore	**Eisenbahnsignal** (n)	['aɪzənba:n zig'nal]
station	**Station** (f)	[ʃta'ʦʲɔ:n]
engineer	**Lokomotivführer** (m)	[lɔkɔmɔ'ti:f 'fy:rə]
porter (of luggage)	**Träger** (m)	['trɛgə]
train steward	**Schaffner** (m)	['ʃafnə]
passenger	**Fahrgast** (m)	['fa:rgast]
conductor	**Fahrkartenkontrolleur** (m)	['fa:rkartən kɔntrɔ'lø:r]
corridor (in train)	**Flur** (m)	[flu:r]
emergency break	**Notbremse** (f)	['nɔ:tbrɛmzə]
compartment	**Abteil** (n)	['aptaɪl]
berth	**Liegeplatz** (m)	['li:gəplaʦ]
upper berth	**oberer Liegeplatz** (m)	['ɔ:bərə 'li:gəplaʦ]
lower berth	**unterer Liegeplatz** (m)	['untərə 'li:gəplaʦ]
bed linen	**Bettwäsche** (f)	['bɛtvəʃə]
ticket	**Fahrkarte** (f)	['fa:rkartə]
schedule	**Zugfahrplan** (m)	[ʦug 'fa:rpla:n]
information display	**Anzeigetafel** (f)	[an'ʦaɪgə 'tafl]
to leave, to depart	**abfahren** (vi)	['apfa:rən]
departure (of train)	**Abfahrt** (f)	['apfa:rt]
to arrive (ab. train)	**ankommen** (vi)	['aŋkɔmən]
arrival	**Ankunft** (f)	['aŋkunft]
to arrive by train	**mit dem Zug kommen**	[mit dem ʦuk 'kɔmən]
to get on the train	**in den Zug einsteigen**	[in den 'ʦuk 'aɪnʃtaɪgən]
to get off the train	**aus dem Zug aussteigen**	[aʊs dem ʦuk 'ausʃtaɪgən]

| train wreck | Zugunglück (n) | ['ʦuːgʊŋ lyk] |
| to be derailed | entgleisen (vi) | [ɛntg'laɪzən] |

steam engine	Dampflok (f)	['dampflɔk]
stoker, fireman	Heizer (m)	['haɪʦə]
firebox	Feuerung (f)	['fɔɪərʊŋ]
coal	Kohle (f)	['kɔːlə]

107. Ship

| ship | Schiff (n) | [ʃif] |
| vessel | Fahrzeug (n) | ['faːrʦɔɪk] |

steamship	Dampfer (m)	['dampfə]
riverboat	Motorschiff (n)	['mɔːtɔːr 'ʃif]
ocean liner	Kreuzfahrtschiff (n)	['krɔɪʦfaːrt ʃif]
cruiser	Kreuzer (m)	['krɔɪʦə]

yacht	Jacht (f)	[jaht]
tugboat	Schlepper (m)	['ʃlɛpə]
barge	Lastkahn (m)	['lastkaːn]
ferry	Fähre (f)	['fɛrə]

sailing ship	Segelschiff (n)	['zeːgl'ʃif]
brigantine	Brigantine (f)	[brigan'tiːnə]
ice breaker	Eisbrecher (m)	['aɪsb'rɛhə]
submarine	U-Boot (n)	['uːbɔːt]

boat (flat-bottomed ~)	Boot (n)	['bɔːt]
dinghy	Dingi (n)	['diŋ i]
lifeboat	Rettungsboot (n)	['rɛtʊŋs bɔːt]
motorboat	Motorboot (n)	['mɔːtɔːr bɔːt]

captain	Kapitän (m)	[kapi'tɛn]
seaman	Matrose (m)	[mat'rɔːzə]
sailor	Seemann (m)	['zeːman]
crew	Besatzung (f)	['bəzaʦʊŋ]

boatswain	Bootsmann (m)	['bɔːʦman]
ship's boy	Schiffsjunge (m)	[ʃifs 'jʊŋə]
cook	Schiffskoch (m)	['ʃifskɔh]
ship's doctor	Schiffsarzt (m)	[ʃifs 'aːrʦt]

deck	Deck (n)	[dɛk]
mast	Mast (m)	[mast]
sail	Segel (n)	['zeːgl]

hold	Schiffsraum (m)	['ʃifs'raum]
bow (prow)	Bug (m)	[bʊk]
stern	Heck (n)	[hɛk]

| oar | Ruder (n) | ['ru:də] |
| screw propeller | Schraube (f) | ['ʃraubə] |

cabin	Kajüte (f)	[ka'ju:tə]
wardroom	Messe (f)	['mɛsə]
engine room	Maschinenraum (m)	[ma'ʃi:nən 'raum]
bridge	Kapitänssteg (m)	[kapi'tɛns ʃtək]
radio room	Funkraum (m)	['fuŋkraum]
wave (radio)	Radiowelle (f)	['ra:dio'vɛlə]
logbook	Schiffstagebuch (n)	['ʃifs'ta:gəbʊh]

spyglass	Fernrohr (n)	['fɛrnrɔ:r]
bell	Glocke (f)	['glɔkə]
flag	Fahne (f)	['fa:nə]

rope (mooring ~)	Seil (n)	[zaɪl]
knot (bowline, etc.)	Knoten (m)	['knɔ:tən]
deckrail	Geländer (n)	['gəlɛndə]
gangway	Treppe (f)	['trɛpə]

anchor	Anker (m)	['aŋkə]
to weigh anchor	den Anker lichten	[den 'aŋkə 'liħtən]
to drop anchor	Anker werfen	['aŋkə 'vɛrfən]
anchor chain	Ankerkette (f)	['aŋkər'ketə]

port (harbor)	Hafen (m)	['ha:fən]
berth, wharf	Anlegestelle (f)	['anle:gəʃ'tɛlə]
to berth (moor)	anlegen (vi)	['anle:gən]
to cast off	abstoßen (vt)	['apʃtɔsən]

trip, voyage	Reise (f)	['raɪzə]
cruise (sea trip)	Kreuzfahrt (f)	['krɔɪtsfa:rt]
course (route)	Kurs (m)	[kʊrs]
route (itinerary)	Reiseroute (f)	['raɪzərʊtə]

fairway	Fahrwasser (n)	['farvasə]
shallows (shoal)	Untiefe (f)	[un'tifə]
to run aground	stranden (vi)	['ʃtrandən]

storm	Sturm (m)	[ʃtʊrm]
signal	Signal (n)	[zig'na:l]
to sink (vi)	untergehen (vi)	['untərge:ən]
Man overboard!	Mann über Bord!	[man 'jubə bɔrt]
SOS	SOS	['ɛs ɔ 'ɛs]
ring buoy	Rettungsring (m)	['rɛtuŋs 'rin]

108. Airport

| airport | Flughafen (m) | ['flykha:fən] |
| airplane | Flugzeug (n) | ['flykts̩ɔɪk] |

| airline | Fluggesellschaft (f) | ['flykɡəzɛlʃaft] |
| air-traffic controller | Fluglotse (m) | ['flyklɔːtsə] |

departure	Abflug (m)	['apflyk]
arrival	Ankunft (f)	['aŋkunft]
to arrive (by plane)	anfliegen (vi)	[anf'liːɡən]

| departure time | Abflugzeit (f) | ['apflyk tsaɪt] |
| arrival time | Ankunftszeit (f) | ['aŋkunfts tsaɪt] |

| to be delayed | sich verspäten | [zɪh fɛrʃ'pɛːtən] |
| flight delay | Abflugverspätung (f) | ['apflyk fɛrʃ'pɛːtuŋ] |

information board	Anzeigetafel (f)	[an'tsaɪɡə 'tafl]
information	Information (f)	[ɪnfɔrma'tsoːn]
to announce (vt)	anzeigen (vt)	['antsaɪɡən]
flight (e.g., next ~)	Flug (m)	[flyk]

| customs | Zollamt (n) | ['tsɔl amt] |
| customs officer | Zollbeamte (m) | ['tsɔl 'beamtə] |

customs declaration	Zollerklärung (f)	[tsɔl ek'lɛːruŋ]
to fill out the declaration	die Zollerklärung ausfüllen	[di 'tsɔlərk'lɛruŋ 'ausfylən]
passport control	Passkontrolle (f)	['paskɔnt'rɔlə]

luggage	Gepäck (n)	['ɡəpɛk]
hand luggage	Handgepäck (n)	['hantɡə'pɛk]
Lost Luggage Desk	Fundbüro (n)	[fɛr'lørenəs ɡə'pɛk byː'rɔː]
luggage cart	Kofferkuli (m)	[kɔfə'kuːli]

landing	Landung (f)	['landuŋ]
landing strip	Landebahn (f)	['landəbaːn]
to land (vi)	landen (vi)	['landən]
airstairs	Fluggasttreppen (pl)	['flykɡastrɛpən]

check-in	Check-in (n)	[tʃɛk 'in]
check-in desk	Check-in-Schalter (m)	[tʃɛk 'in 'ʃaltə]
to check-in (vi)	sich registrieren lassen	[zɪh regist'riːrən 'lasən]
boarding pass	Bordkarte (f)	['bɔrtkartə]
departure gate	Abfluggate (n)	['apflyk 'ɡatə]

transit	Transit (m)	[tran'ziːt]
to wait (vt)	warten (vi)	['vartən]
departure lounge	Wartesaal (m)	['vartəzaːl]
to see off	begleiten (vt)	['bəɡlaɪtən]
to say goodbye	sich verabschieden	[zɪh fɛrap'ʃiːdən]

Life events

109. Holidays. Event

celebration, holiday	**Fest** (n)	[fɛst]
national day	**Nationalfeiertag** (m)	[natsɪoˈnaːl ˈfajertag]
public holiday	**Feiertag** (m)	[ˈfajertaːk]
to commemorate (vt)	**feiern** (vt)	[ˈfaɪərn]
event (happening)	**Ereignis** (n)	[ɛˈraɪgnis]
event (organized activity)	**Veranstaltung** (f)	[fɛranʃˈtaltʊŋ]
banquet (party)	**Bankett** (n)	[baˈŋkɛt]
reception (formal party)	**Empfang** (m)	[ɛmpˈfaŋ]
feast	**Festmahl** (n)	[ˈfɛstmaːl]
anniversary	**Jahrestag** (m)	[ˈjarəstaːk]
jubilee	**Jubiläumsfeier** (f)	[jubiˈlɛːums ˈfaɪə]
to celebrate (vt)	**begehen** (vt)	[ˈbəgeːən]
New Year	**Neujahr** (n)	[ˈnɔjaːr]
Happy New Year!	**Frohes Neues Jahr!**	[ˈfrɔəs ˈnɔɪəs jaːr]
Christmas	**Weihnachten** (n)	[ˈvaɪnahtən]
Merry Christmas!	**Frohe Weihnachten!**	[ˈfrɔə ˈvaɪnahtən]
Christmas tree	**Tannenbaum** (m)	[ˈtanənˈbaum]
fireworks	**Feuerwerk** (n)	[ˈfɔɪəvɛrk]
wedding	**Hochzeit** (f)	[ˈhɔhˈtsaɪt]
groom	**Bräutigam** (m)	[ˈbrɔɪtigam]
bride	**Braut** (f)	[ˈbraut]
to invite (vt)	**einladen** (vt)	[ˈaɪnladən]
invitation card	**Einladung** (f)	[ˈaɪnlaːdʊŋ]
guest	**Gast** (m)	[gast]
to visit	**besuchen** (vt)	[ˈbəzuːhən]
(~ your parents, etc.)		
to greet the guests	**Gäste empfangen**	[ˈgɛstə ɛmpˈfaŋən]
gift, present	**Geschenk** (n)	[ˈgəʃɛŋk]
to give (sth as present)	**schenken** (vt)	[ˈʃɛŋkən]
to receive gifts	**Geschenke bekommen**	[ˈgəʃɛŋkə ˈbəkɔmən]
bouquet (of flowers)	**Blumenstrauß** (m)	[ˈbluːmənʃtraus]
congratulations	**Glückwunsch** (m)	[ˈglykvʊnʃ]
to congratulate (vt)	**gratulieren** (vi)	[gratuˈliːrən]

greeting card	Glückwunschkarte (f)	['glykvʊnʃ 'kartə]
to send a postcard	eine Karte abschicken	['aɪnə 'kartə 'apʃɪkən]
to get a postcard	eine Karte erhalten	['aɪnə 'kartə 'ərhaltən]
toast	Trinkspruch (m)	['trɪŋkʃprʊh]
to offer (a drink, etc.)	bewirten (vt)	['bəwɪrtən]
champagne	Champagner (m)	[ʃam'paɲə]
to have fun	sich amüsieren	[zɪɦ amy'ziːrən]
fun, merriment	Fröhlichkeit (f)	['frøːlɪɦkaɪt]
joy (emotion)	Freude (f)	['frɔɪdə]
ΠΠΠθθ	Tanz (m)	[tants]
to dance (vi, vt)	tanzen (vi, vt)	['tantsən]
waltz	Walzer (m)	['valtsə]
tango	Tango (m)	['taŋ ɔ]

110. Funerals. Burial

cemetery	Friedhof (m)	['friːthɔf]
grave, tomb	Grab (n)	[graːp]
gravestone	Grabstein (m)	['graːpʃtaɪn]
fence	Zaun (m)	['tsaun]
chapel	Kapelle (f)	[ka'pɛlə]
death	Tod (m)	[tɔt]
to die (vi)	sterben (vi)	['ʃtɛrbn]
the deceased	Verstorbene (m)	[fɛrʃ'tɔrbənə]
mourning	Trauer (f)	['trauə]
to bury (vt)	begraben (vt)	['bəgraːbn]
funeral home	Bestattungsanstalt (f)	['bəʃtatʊŋs 'anʃtalt]
funeral	Begräbnis (n)	['bəgrɛbnis]
wreath	Kranz (m)	[krants]
casket	Sarg (m)	[zark]
hearse	Katafalk (m)	[kata'falk]
shroud	Totenhemd (n)	['tɔtənhəmt]
funeral procession	Trauerzug (m)	['trauətsuk]
cremation urn	Urne (f)	['urnə]
crematory	Krematorium (n)	[krema'tɔːrium]
obituary	Nachruf (m)	['naːhruːf]
to cry (weep)	weinen (vi)	['vaɪnən]
to sob (vi)	schluchzen (vi)	['ʃluhtsən]

111. War. Soldiers

platoon	**Zug** (m)	[ʦuk]
company	**Kompanie** (f)	[kɔmpa'ni:]
regiment	**Regiment** (n)	[regi'mɛnt]
army	**Armee** (f)	[ar'me:]
division	**Division** (f)	[diwi'zʹɔ:n]
section, squad	**Abteilung** (f)	['aptaɪluŋ]
host (army)	**Heer** (n)	['he:ə]
soldier	**Soldat** (m)	[zɔl'da:t]
officer	**Offizier** (m)	[ɔfi'ʦi:ə]
private	**Soldat** (m)	[zɔl'da:t]
sergeant	**Feldwebel** (m)	['feltwe:bl]
lieutenant	**Leutnant** (m)	['lɔɪtnant]
captain	**Hauptmann** (m)	['hauptman]
major	**Major** (m)	[ma'jɔ:r]
colonel	**Oberst** (m)	['ɔ:bərst]
general	**General** (m)	[genə'ra:l]
sailor	**Matrose** (m)	[mat'rɔ:zə]
captain	**Kapitän** (m)	[kapi'tɛn]
boatswain	**Bootsmann** (m)	['bɔ:ʦman]
artilleryman	**Artillerist** (m)	[artile'rist]
paratrooper	**Fallschirmjäger** (m)	['falʃirm 'je:gə]
pilot	**Pilot** (m)	[pi'lo:t]
navigator	**Steuermann** (m)	['ʃtɔɪəman]
mechanic	**Mechaniker** (m)	[me'ha:nikə]
pioneer (sapper)	**Pionier** (m)	[piɔ'ni:ə]
parachutist	**Fallschirmspringer** (m)	['falʃirm 'ʃpriŋə]
reconnaissance scout	**Aufklärer** (m)	['aufk'lerə]
sniper	**Scharfschütze** (m)	['ʃarf'ʃyʦə]
patrol (group)	**Patrouille** (f)	[pat'rʊlə]
to patrol (vt)	**patrouillieren** (vi)	[patrʊ'li:rən]
sentry, guard	**Wache** (f)	['vahə]
warrior	**Krieger** (m)	['kri:gə]
hero	**Held** (m)	[hɛlt]
heroine	**Heldin** (f)	['hɛldin]
patriot	**Patriot** (m)	[patri'ɔ:t]
traitor	**Verräter** (m)	[fɛ'rɛ:tə]
to betray (vt)	**verraten** (vt)	[fɛ'ra:tən]
deserter	**Deserteur** (m)	[dezər'tø:r]
to desert (vi)	**desertieren** (vi)	[dezər'ti:rən]

mercenary	**Söldner** (m)	['zøldnə]
recruit	**Rekrut** (m)	[rek'rʊ:t]
volunteer	**Freiwillige** (m)	['fraɪwiligə]

dead (n)	**Ermordete** (m)	[ɛr'mɔrdetə]
wounded (n)	**Verwundete** (m)	[fɛr'vʊndetə]
prisoner of war	**Kriegsgefangene** (m)	[kri:ks gə'fa:ŋenə]

112. War. Military actions. Part 1

war	**Krieg** (m)	[kɪl.k]
to be at war	**Krieg führen**	[kri:k 'fy:rən]
civil war	**Bürgerkrieg** (m)	['byrgərkrik]

treacherously (adv)	**heimtückisch**	['haɪmtykiʃ]
declaration of war	**Kriegserklärung** (f)	['kriks ɛrk'lɛrʊŋ]
to declare (~ war)	**erklären** (vt)	[ɛrk'lerən]
aggression	**Aggression** (f)	[agrə'sʲɔ:n]
to attack (invade)	**einfallen** (vt)	['a:ɪnfa:lən]

to invade (vt)	**in ... einfallen** (vi)	[in 'aɪnfalən]
invader	**Invasoren** (pl)	[inva'zɔ:rən]
conqueror	**Eroberer** (m)	[ɛ'rɔ:bərə]

defense	**Verteidigung** (f)	[fɛr'taɪdigʊŋ]
to defend (a country, etc.)	**verteidigen** (vt)	[fɛr'taɪdigən]
to defend oneself	**sich verteidigen**	[ziɦ fɛr'taɪdigən]

enemy	**Feind** (m)	[faɪnt]
foe, adversary	**Gegner** (m)	['gɛgnə]
enemy (as adj)	**Feind-**	[faɪnt]

| strategy | **Strategie** (f) | [ʃtratə'gi:] |
| tactics | **Taktik** (f) | ['taktik] |

order	**Befehl** (m)	['befe:l]
command (order)	**Anordnung** (f)	[a'nordnʊŋ]
to order (vt)	**befehlen** (vt)	['befe:lən]
mission	**Auftrag** (m)	['auftra:k]
secret (adj)	**geheim**	['gəhaɪm]

| battle | **Gefecht** (n) | [ge'fɛɦt] |
| combat | **Kampf** (m) | [kampf] |

attack	**Angriff** (m)	['aŋ rif]
storming (assault)	**Sturm** (m)	[ʃtʊrm]
to storm (vt)	**stürmen** (vt)	['ʃtyrmən]
siege (to be under ~)	**Belagerung** (f)	['bəlagerʊŋ]
offensive (n)	**Angriff** (m)	['aŋ rif]
to go on the offensive	**angreifen** (vt)	['aŋ raɪfən]

retreat	**Rückzug** (m)	['ryktsuk]
to retreat (vi)	**sich zurückziehen**	[ziħ tsu'ryktsi:ən]
encirclement	**Einkesselung** (f)	[aɪ'ŋkɛselʊŋ]
to encircle (vt)	**einkesseln** (vt)	[aɪ'ŋkɛ:səln]
bombing (by aircraft)	**Bombenangriff** (m)	['bɔmbən 'aŋ rif]
to drop a bomb	**eine Bombe abwerfen**	['aɪnə 'bɔmbə 'apvərfən]
to bomb (vt)	**bombardieren** (vt)	[bɔmbar'di:rən]
explosion	**Explosion** (f)	[ɛksplo'z'ɔ:n]
shot	**Schuss** (m)	[ʃʊs]
to fire a shot	**schießen** (vt)	['ʃi:sən]
firing (burst of ~)	**Schießerei** (f)	[ʃi:sə'raɪ]
to take aim (at …)	**zielen auf …**	['tsi:lən 'auf]
to point (a gun)	**richten** (vt)	['riħtən]
to hit (the target)	**treffen** (vt)	['trɛfən]
to sink (~ a ship)	**versenken** (vt)	[fɛr'zɛŋkən]
hole (in a ship)	**Loch** (n)	['lɔh]
to founder, to sink (vi)	**versinken** (vi)	[fɛr'ziŋkən]
front (war ~)	**Front** (f)	[frɔnt]
rear (homefront)	**Hinterland** (n)	['hintə lant]
evacuation	**Evakuierung** (f)	[ɛvakʊ'i:rʊŋ]
to evacuate (vt)	**evakuieren** (vt)	[ɛvakʊ'i:rən]
barbwire	**Stacheldraht** (m)	['ʃtaheldra:t]
barrier (anti tank ~)	**Sperre** (f)	['ʃpɛrə]
watchtower	**Wachtturm** (m)	['vahtʊrm]
hospital	**Lazarett** (n)	[laza'rɛt]
to wound (vt)	**verwunden** (vt)	[fɛr'vʊndən]
wound	**Wunde** (f)	['vʊndə]
wounded (n)	**Verwundete** (m)	[fɛr'vʊndətə]
to be wounded	**verletzt sein**	[fɛr'le:tst zaɪn]
serious (wound)	**schwer**	[ʃwe:ə]

113. War. Military actions. Part 2

captivity	**Gefangenschaft** (f)	['gəfaŋənʃaft]
to take captive	**gefangen nehmen** (vt)	['gəfaŋən 'ne:mən]
to be in captivity	**in Gefangenschaft sein**	[in 'gəfaŋənʃaft zaɪn]
to be taken prisoner	**in Gefangenschaft geraten**	[in 'gəfaŋənʃaft gəratən]
concentration camp	**Konzentrationslager** (n)	[kɔntsɛntra'tsʲɔ:ns 'la:gə]
prisoner of war	**Kriegsgefangene** (m)	[kri:ks gə'fa:ŋenə]
to escape (vi)	**fliehen** (vi)	['fli:ən]

to betray (vt)	verraten (vt)	[fɛ'ra:tən]
betrayer	Verräter (m)	[fɛ'rɛ:tə]
betrayal	Verrat (m)	[fɛ'ra:t]
to execute (shoot)	erschießen (vt)	[ɛr'ʃi:sən]
execution (by firing squad)	Erschießung (f)	[ɛr'ʃi:sʊŋ]
equipment (military gear)	Ausrüstung (f)	[aʊs'rystʊŋ]
shoulder board	Schulterstück (n)	['ʃʊltəʃtyk]
gas mask	Gasmaske (f)	[ga:s'maskə]
radio transmitter	Funkgerät (n)	['fʊŋkgə'rɛt]
cipher, code	Chiffre (f)	['ʃifrə]
secrecy	Konspiration (f)	[kɔnspira'tsjo:n]
password	Kennwort (n)	['kɛnvɔrt]
land mine	Mine (f)	['mi:nə]
to mine (road, etc.)	Minen legen	['mi:nən 'le:gən]
minefield	Minenfeld (n)	['mi:nən'fɛlt]
air-raid warning	Luftalarm (m)	['lyft alarm]
alarm (warning)	Alarm (m)	[ala:rm]
signal	Signal (n)	[zig'na:l]
signal flare	Signalrakete (f)	[zig'na:l ra'ke:tə]
headquarters	Stab (m)	[ʃtap]
reconnaissance	Aufklärung (f)	[aɪfk'lerʊŋ]
situation	Lage (f)	['la:gə]
report	Bericht (m)	['bəriht]
ambush	Hinterhalt (m)	['hintə halt]
reinforcement (of army)	Verstärkung (f)	[fɛrʃ'tɛrkʊŋ]
target	Zielscheibe (f)	['tsi:lʃaɪbə]
proving ground	Schießplatz (m)	['ʃi:splats]
military exercise	Manöver (n)	[ma'nø:və]
panic	Panik (f)	['pa:nik]
devastation	Verwüstung (f)	[fɛr'wy:stʊŋ]
destruction, ruins	Trümmer (pl)	['trymə]
to destroy (vt)	zerstören (vt)	['tsɛrʃtø:rən]
to survive (vi, vt)	überleben (vi)	['ju:bər'le:bn]
to disarm (vt)	entwaffnen (vt)	[ɛnt'vafnən]
to handle (~ a gun)	handhaben (vt)	[na:nt'ha:bn]
Attention!	Stillgestanden!	['ʃtilgəʃtandən]
At ease!	Rühren!	['ry:rən]
feat (of courage)	Heldentat (f)	['hɛldəntat]
oath (vow)	Eid (m), Schwur (m)	[aɪt], [ʃvu:r]
to swear (an oath)	schwören (vi, vt)	['ʃwø:rən]
decoration (medal, etc.)	Lohn (m)	[lo:n]

to award (give medal to)	**auszeichnen** (vt)	['aus'tsaɪɦnən]
medal	**Medaille** (f)	[me'daʎə]
order (e.g., ~ of Merit)	**Orden** (m)	['ɔrdən]

victory	**Sieg** (m)	[zlːk]
defeat	**Niederlage** (f)	['niːdərlaːgə]
armistice	**Waffenstillstand** (m)	['vafənʃ'tilʃtant]

banner (standard)	**Fahne** (f)	['faːnə]
glory (honor, fame)	**Ruhm** (m)	[rʊːm]
parade	**Parade** (f)	[pa'raːdə]
to march (on parade)	**marschieren** (vi)	[mar'ʃiːrən]

114. Weapons

weapons	**Waffe** (f)	['vafə]
firearm	**Schusswaffe** (f)	['ʃusvafə]
cold weapons (knives, etc.)	**blanke Waffe** (f)	['blaŋkə 'vafə]

chemical weapons	**chemischen Waffen** (pl)	['heːmiʃən 'vafən]
nuclear (adj)	**Kern-, Atom-**	[kɛrn], [a'tɔm]
nuclear weapons	**Kernwaffe** (f)	['kɛrnvafə]

| bomb | **Bombe** (f) | ['bɔmbə] |
| atomic bomb | **Atombombe** (f) | [a'tɔːm 'bɔmbə] |

pistol (gun)	**Pistole** (f)	[pis'toːlə]
rifle	**Gewehr** (n)	['gəvɛr]
submachine gun	**Maschinenpistole** (f)	[ma'ʃiːnən pis'toːlə]
machine gun	**Maschinengewehr** (n)	[ma'ʃiːnən 'gəweːr]

muzzle	**Mündung** (f)	['myndʊŋ]
barrel	**Lauf** (m)	['lauf]
caliber	**Kaliber** (n)	[ka'liːbə]

trigger	**Abzug** (m)	['aptsuk]
sight (aiming device)	**Visier** (n)	['wiːziə]
magazine	**Magazin** (n)	[maga'tsiːn]
butt (of rifle)	**Kolben** (m)	[kɔlbən]

| hand grenade | **Granate** (f) | [gra'naːtə] |
| explosive | **Sprengstoff** (m) | ['ʃprɛnʃtɔf] |

bullet	**Kugel** (f)	['kʊːgl]
cartridge	**Patrone** (f)	[pat'rɔːnə]
charge	**Ladung** (f)	['ladʊŋ]
ammunition	**Munition** (f)	[mʊni'tsɔːn]
bomber (aircraft)	**Bomber** (m)	['bɔmbə]
fighter	**Kampfflugzeug** (n)	['kampf'lyktsɔɪk]

helicopter	Hubschrauber (m)	['hʊrʃraubə]
anti-aircraft gun	Flugabwehrkanone (f)	['flykabvə ka'nɔ:nə]
tank	Panzer (m)	['pantsə]
tank gun	Panzerkanone (f)	['pantsə ka:'nɔnə]

| artillery | Artillerie (f) | [artile'ri:] |
| to lay (a gun) | richten (vt) | ['riftən] |

shell (projectile)	Geschoß (n)	['gəʃɔs]
mortar bomb	Wurfgranate (f)	[vʊ:rf gra'na:tə]
mortar	Granatwerfer (m)	[gra'na·t'ırrfə]
splinter (shell fragment)	Splitter (m)	[ʃplitə]

submarine	U-Boot (n)	['u:bo:t]
torpedo	Torpedo (m)	[tɔr'pɛdɔ]
missile	Rakete (f)	[ra'ke:tə]

to load (gun)	laden (vt)	['la:dən]
to shoot (vi)	schießen (vi)	['ʃi:sən]
to point at (the cannon)	zielen auf ...	['tsi:lən 'auf]
bayonet	Bajonett (n)	[bajɔ'nɛt]

epee	Degen (m)	['de:gən]
saber (e.g., cavalry ~)	Säbel (m)	['zɛ:bl]
spear (weapon)	Speer (m)	['ʃpe:ə]
bow	Bogen (m)	['bo:gən]
arrow	Pfeil (m)	[pfaıl]
musket	Muskete (f)	[mʊs'kɛ:tə]
crossbow	Armbrust (f)	['armb'rʊst]

115. Ancient people

primitive (prehistoric)	ursprünglich	['u:rʃp'ryŋliħ]
prehistoric (adj)	prähistorisch	['prɛhisto:riʃ]
ancient (~ civilization)	alt	[alt]

Stone Age	Steinzeit (f)	['ʃtaıntsaıt]
Bronze Age	Bronzezeit (f)	['brɔntsetsaıt]
Ice Age	Eiszeit (f)	['aıstsaıt]

tribe	Stamm (m)	[ʃtam]
cannibal	Kannibale (m)	[kani'balə]
hunter	Jäger (m)	['je:gə]
to hunt (vi, vt)	jagen (vi)	['jagən]
mammoth	Mammut (n)	[ma'mʊt]

cave	Höhle (f)	['hø:lə]
fire	Feuer (n)	['fɔıə]
campfire	Lagerfeuer (n)	['la:gə 'fɔıə]
rock painting	Höhlenmalerei (f)	['hø:lən ma:lə'raı]

tool (e.g., stone ax)	Werkzeug (n)	['vɛrktsɔɪk]
spear	Speer (m)	['ʃpeːə]
stone ax	Steinbeil (n)	['ʃtaɪn 'baɪl]
to be at war	Krieg führen	[kriːk 'fyːrən]
to domesticate (vt)	domestizieren (vt)	[dɔmɛsti'tsiːrən]

idol	Idol (n)	[i'dɔːl]
to worship (vt)	anbeten (vt)	[anbeten vt]
superstition	Aberglaube (m)	['aːbərglaubə]

evolution	Evolution (f)	[ɛvɔly'tsɪɔːn]
development	Entwicklung (f)	[ɛnt'wiklun]
disappearance (extinction)	Verschwinden (n)	[fɛrʃ'windən]
to adapt oneself	sich anpassen	[ziħ an'pasn]

archeology	Archäologie (f)	[arheɔlɔ'giː]
archeologist	Archäologe (m)	[arheɔ'lɔːgə]
archeological (adj)	archäologisch	[arheɔ'lɔːgiʃ]

excavation site	Ausgrabungsstätte (pl)	[ausg'raːbuŋs 'ʃtɛtə]
excavations	Ausgrabungen (pl)	[ausg'raːbuŋən]
find (object)	Fund (m)	[funt]
fragment	Fragment (n)	[frag'mɛnt]

116. Middle Ages

people (ethnic group)	Volk (n)	[fɔlk]
peoples	Völker (pl)	['følkə]
tribe	Stamm (m)	[ʃtam]
tribes	Stämme (pl)	['ʃtɛːmə]

barbarians	Barbaren (pl)	[bar'baːrən]
Gauls	Gallier (pl)	['galiə]
Goths	Goten (pl)	['gotən]
Slavs	Slawen (pl)	['slavən]
Vikings	Wikinger (pl)	['wiːkiŋə]

| Romans | Römer (pl) | ['røːmə] |
| Roman (adj) | römisch | ['rømiʃ] |

Byzantines	Byzantiner (pl)	[bytsan'tinə]
Byzantium	Byzanz (n)	[by'tsanfs]
Byzantine (adj)	byzantinisch	[bytsan'tiːniʃ]

emperor	Kaiser (m)	['kaɪzə]
leader, chief	Häuptling (m)	['hɔɪptliŋ]
powerful (~ king)	mächtig	['mɛħtiħ]
king	König (m)	['køːniħ]
ruler (sovereign)	Herrscher (m)	['hɛrʃə]
knight	Ritter (m)	['ritə]

feudal lord	Feudalherr (m)	['fɔɪdalher]
feudal (adj)	feudal, Feudal-	[fɔɪ'dal]
vassal	Vasall (m)	[fa'sal]

duke	Herzog (m)	['hɛrtsɔːk]
earl	Graf (m)	[graf]
baron	Baron (m)	[ba'rɔn]
bishop	Bischof (m)	['bɪʃɔf]

armor	Rüstung (f)	['rystʊŋ]
shield	Schild (m)	[ʃɪlt]
sword	Schwert (n)	[ʃweːrt]
visor	Visier (n)	['wiːziə]
chainmail	Panzerhemd (n)	['pantsə hemt]

| crusade | Kreuzzug (m) | ['krɔɪts tsuk] |
| crusader | Kreuzritter (m) | ['krɔɪtsritə] |

| territory | Territorium (n) | [tɛri'toːrium] |
| to attack (invade) | einfallen (vt) | ['aːɪnfaːlən] |

| to conquer (vt) | erobern (vt) | [ɛ'rɔːbərn] |
| to occupy (invade) | besetzen (vt) | ['bəzɛːtsn] |

siege (to be under ~)	Belagerung (f)	['bəlagərʊŋ]
besieged (adj)	belagert	['bəlagərt]
to besiege (vt)	belagern (vt)	['bəlagərn]

inquisition	Inquisition (f)	[iŋkwizi'tsʲɔːn]
inquisitor	Inquisitor (m)	[iŋkwizi'tɔːr]
torture	Folter (f)	['fɔltə]
cruel (adj)	grausam	['grauzam]

| heretic | Häretiker (m) | [hɛ'retikə] |
| heresy | Häresie (f) | [hɛre'ziː] |

seafaring	Seefahrt (f)	['zeːfaːrt]
pirate	Seeräuber (m)	['zeː'rɔɪbə]
piracy	Seeräuberei (f)	['zeː'rɔɪbəraɪ]
boarding (attack)	Enterung (f)	['ɛnterʊŋ]

| loot, booty | Beute (f) | ['bɔɪtə] |
| treasures | Schätze (pl) | ['ʃɛtsə] |

discovery	Entdeckung (f)	[ɛnt'dɛkʊŋ]
to discover (new land, etc.)	entdecken (vt)	[ɛnt'dɛkən]
expedition	Expedition (f)	[ɛkspedi'tsʲɔːn]

musketeer	Musketier (m)	[mʊsketiə]
cardinal	Kardinal (m)	[kardi'naːl]
heraldry	Heraldik (f)	[he'raldik]
heraldic (adj)	heraldisch	[he'raldiʃ]

117. Leader. Chief. Authorities

king	König (m)	['køːniħ]
queen	Königin (f)	['køːnigin]
royal (adj)	königlich	['køːnigliħ]
kingdom	Königreich (n)	[køːniħ'raıħ]

| prince | Prinz (m) | [prints] |
| princess | Prinzessin (f) | [prin'tsɛsin] |

president	Präsident (m)	[prɛzi'dɛnt]
vice-president	Vizepräsident (m)	['witsə prɛzi'dɛnt]
senator	Senator (m)	[ze'naːtɔːr]

monarch	Monarch (m)	[mɔ'narh]
ruler (sovereign)	Führer (m)	['fyːrə]
dictator	Diktator (m)	[dik'taːtɔːr]
tyrant	Tyrann (m)	[ty'ran]
magnate	Magnat (m)	[mag'naːt]

director	Direktor (m)	[di'rɛktɔːr]
chief	Chef (m)	[ʃɛf]
manager (director)	Leiter (m)	['laıtə]
boss	Boss (m)	[bɔs]
owner	Wirt (m)	[wirt]

head (~ of delegation)	Leiter (m)	['laıtə]
authorities	Behörden (pl)	['bəhørdən]
superiors	Vorgesetzten (pl)	['fɔːrgə'zɛtstən]

governor	Gouverneur (m)	[gʊːvɛr'nøːr]
consul	Konsul (m)	['kɔnzul]
diplomat	Diplomat (m)	[diplɔ'maːt]
mayor	Bürgermeister (m)	['byrgərmaıstə]
sheriff	Sheriff (m)	[ʃɛ'rif]

emperor	Kaiser (m)	['kaızə]
tsar, czar	Zar (m)	[tsaːr]
pharaoh	Pharao (m)	[faː'raɔ]
khan	Khan (m)	[kan]

118. Breaking the law. Criminals. Part 1

bandit	Bandit (m)	[ban'diːt]
crime	Verbrechen (n)	[fɛrb'rɛhn]
criminal (person)	Verbrecher (m)	[fɛrb'rɛhə]

| thief | Dieb (m) | [diːp] |
| to steal (vi, vt) | stehlen (vt) | ['ʃteːlən] |

stealing (larceny)	**Diebstahl** (m)	['di:pʃta:l]
theft	**Stehlen** (n)	['ʃte:lən]
to kidnap (vt)	**kidnappen** (vt)	['kitnəpən]
kidnapping	**Kidnapping** (n)	['kitnəpiŋ]
kidnapper	**Kidnapper** (m)	['kitnəpə]
ransom	**Lösegeld** (n)	[løːzə'gɛlt]
to demand ransom	**Lösegeld verlangen**	[løːzə'gɛlt fɛr'laŋən]
to rob (vt)	**rauben** (vt)	['raubn]
robbery	**Raub** (m)	['raup]
robber	**Räuber** (m)	['rɔıbə]
to extort (vt)	**erpressen** (vt)	[ɛrp'rɛsn]
extortionist	**Erpresser** (m)	[ɛrp'rɛsə]
extortion	**Erpressung** (f)	[ɛrp'rɛsʊŋ]
to murder, to kill	**morden** (vt)	['mɔːrdən]
murder	**Mord** (m)	[mɔrt]
murderer	**Mörder** (m)	['mørdə]
gunshot	**Schuss** (m)	[ʃʊs]
to fire a shot	**schießen** (vt)	['ʃiːsən]
to shoot to death	**erschießen** (vt)	[ɛr'ʃiːsən]
to shoot (vi)	**schießen** (vi)	['ʃiːsən]
shooting	**Schießerei** (f)	[ʃiːsə'raı]
incident (fight, etc.)	**Vorfall** (m)	['fɔːrfal]
fight, brawl	**Schlägerei** (f)	[ʃlɛgə'raı]
victim	**Opfer** (n)	['ɔpfə]
to damage (vt)	**beschädigen** (vt)	['bəʃɛːdigən]
damage	**Schaden** (m)	['ʃaːdən]
dead body	**Leiche** (f)	['laıhə]
grave (~ crime)	**schwer**	[ʃweːə]
to attack (vt)	**angreifen** (vt)	['aŋ raıfən]
to beat (dog, person)	**schlagen** (vt)	['ʃlaːgən]
to beat up	**verprügeln** (vt)	[fɛrp'rygəln]
to take (rob of sth)	**wegnehmen** (vt)	['vɛkneːmən]
to stab to death	**erstechen** (vt)	[ɛrʃ'tchn]
to maim (vt)	**verstümmeln** (vt)	[fɛrʃtyməln]
to wound (vt)	**verwunden** (vt)	[fɛr'vʊndən]
blackmail	**Erpressung** (f)	[ɛrp'rɛsʊŋ]
to blackmail (vt)	**erpressen** (vt)	[ɛrp'rɛsn]
blackmailer	**Erpresser** (m)	[ɛrp'rɛsə]
protection racket	**Schutzgelderpressung** (f)	['ʃʊtsgɛʎt ɛrp'rɛsʊŋ]
racketeer	**Erpresser** (m)	[ɛrp'rɛsə]
gangster	**Gangster** (m)	['gɛŋstə]

mafia, Mob	**Mafia** (f)	[ˈmaːfia]
pickpocket	**Taschendieb** (m)	[ˈtaʃənˈdiːp]
burglar	**Einbrecher** (m)	[ˈaɪnbrəhə]
smuggling	**Schmuggel** (m)	[ˈʃmʊːgl]
smuggler	**Schmuggler** (m)	[ˈʃmʊːglə]
forgery	**Fälschung** (f)	[ˈfɛlʃʊŋ]
to forge (counterfeit)	**fälschen** (vt)	[ˈfɛlʃn]
fake (forged)	**gefälscht**	[gəˈfɛlʃt]

119. Breaking the law. Criminals. Part 2

rape	**Vergewaltigung** (f)	[fɛrgəˈvaltigʊŋ]
to rape (vt)	**vergewaltigen** (vt)	[fɛrgəˈvaltigən]
rapist	**Gewalttäter** (m)	[ˈgəvaltɛtə]
maniac	**Besessene** (m)	[beˈzɛsənə]
prostitute (fem.)	**Prostituierte** (f)	[prɔstituˈiːrtə]
prostitution	**Prostitution** (f)	[prɔstituˈtsʲɔn]
pimp	**Zuhälter** (m)	[ˈtsuhɛltə]
drug addict	**Drogenabhängiger** (m)	[ˈdrɔːgən ˈaphɛŋigə]
drug dealer	**Drogenhändler** (m)	[ˈdrɔgən ˈhɛndlə]
to blow up (bomb)	**sprengen** (vt)	[ˈʃprɛŋən]
explosion	**Explosion** (f)	[ɛksplɔˈzʲɔːn]
to set fire	**in Brand stecken**	[in brant ˈʃtɛkən]
incendiary (arsonist)	**Brandstifter** (m)	[ˈbrantʃtiːftə]
terrorism	**Terrorismus** (m)	[tɛrɔˈrismʊs]
terrorist	**Terrorist** (m)	[tɛrɔˈrist]
hostage	**Geisel** (f)	[ˈgaɪzl]
to swindle (vt)	**betrügen** (vt)	[ˈbətryːgən]
swindle	**Betrug** (m)	[ˈbətrʊːk]
swindler	**Betrüger** (m)	[ˈbətryːgə]
to bribe (vt)	**bestechen** (vt)	[ˈbəʃtɛhn]
bribery	**Bestechlichkeit** (f)	[ˈbəʃtɛhlikaɪt]
bribe	**Bestechungsgeld** (n)	[ˈbəʃtəhʊŋsgelt]
poison	**Gift** (n)	[gift]
to poison (vt)	**vergiften** (vt)	[fɛrˈgiftən]
to poison oneself	**sich vergiften**	[ziɦ fɛrˈgiftən]
suicide (act)	**Selbstmord** (m)	[ˈzɛlpstmɔrt]
suicide (person)	**Selbstmörder** (m), **-in** (f)	[ˈzɛlpstmørdə], [rin]
to threaten (vt)	**drohen** (vi)	[ˈdrɔːən]
threat	**Drohung** (f)	[ˈdrɔʊŋ]

to make an attempt	versuchen (vt)	[fɛr'zu:hən]
attempt (attack)	Attentat (n)	['atəntat]
to steal (a car)	stehlen (vt)	['ʃte:lən]
to hijack (a plane)	entführen (vt)	[ɛnt'fy:rən]
revenge	Rache (f)	['rahə]
to revenge (vt)	sich rächen	[ziħ 'rɛhən]
to torture (vt)	foltern (vt)	['fɔːltərn]
torture	Folter (f)	['fɔltə]
to torment (vt)	quälen (vt)	['kvɛlən]
pirate	Seeräuber (m)	['ze:'rɔɪbə]
hooligan	Rowdy (m)	['rɔudi]
armed (adj)	bewaffnet	['bəvafnət]
violence	Gewalt (f)	['gəvalt]
spying (n)	Spionage (f)	[ʃpiɔ'na:ʒə]
to spy (vi)	spionieren (vi)	[ʃpiɔ'ni:rən]

120. Police. Law. Part 1

justice	Justiz (f)	[jus'ti:ts]
court (court room)	Gericht (n)	['gəriħt]
judge	Richter (m)	['riħtə]
jurors	Geschworenen (pl)	['gəʃvɔ:rənən]
jury trial	Geschworenengericht (n)	['gəʃvɔ:rənəŋ əriħt]
to judge (vt)	richten (vt)	['riħtən]
lawyer, attorney	Rechtsanwalt (m)	['rɛħ'tsanvalt]
accused	Angeklagte (m)	['aŋ əkla:ktə]
dock	Anklagebank (f)	['aŋkla:gə'baŋk]
charge	Anklage (f)	['aŋkla:gə]
accused	Beschuldigte (m)	[bəʃʊl'diħtə]
sentence	Urteil (n)	['urtaɪl]
to sentence (vt)	verurteilen (vt)	[fɛ'rʊ:rtaɪlən]
guilty (culprit)	Schuldige (m)	['ʃʊldigə]
to punish (vt)	bestrafen (vt)	['bəʃtra:fən]
punishment	Strafe (f)	['ʃtra:fə]
fine (penalty)	Geldstrafe (f)	['gɛlt 'ʃtra:fə]
life imprisonment	lebenslange Haft (f)	['le:bəns'laŋə haft]
death penalty	Todesstrafe (f)	['tɔ:dəsʃt'ra:fə]
electric chair	elektrischer Stuhl (m)	[ɛ'lektriʃə ʃtʊ:l]
gallows	Galgen (m)	['galgən]

| to execute (vt) | hinrichten (vt) | ['hinrɪçtən] |
| execution | Hinrichtung (f) | ['hinrɪçtʊŋ] |

| prison, jail | Gefängnis (n) | [gəˈfɛŋis] |
| cell | Zelle (f) | ['tsɛlə] |

escort	Eskorte (f)	[ɛsˈkɔrtə]
prison guard	Gefängniswärter (m)	[gəˈfɛŋis ˈvɛːrtə]
prisoner	Gefangene (m)	[gəfaŋənə]

| handcuffs | Handschellen (pl) | ['hantˌʃɛlən] |
| to handcuff (vt) | Handschellen anlegen | ['hantˌʃɛlən 'anleːgən] |

prison break	Ausbruch (m)	['ausbrʊh]
to break out (vi)	ausbrechen (vi)	[ausbˈrɛhn]
to disappear (vi)	verschwinden (vi)	[fɛrˈʃwindən]
to release (from prison)	aus … entlassen	[aus ɛntˈlasn]
amnesty	Amnestie (f)	[amnəsˈtiː]

police	Polizei (f)	[poliˈtsaɪ]
police officer	Polizist (m)	[poliˈtsist]
police station	Polizeiwache (f)	[poliˈtsaɪ ˈvahə]
billy club	Gummiknüppel (m)	['gymikˈnyːpl]
bullhorn	Sprachrohr (n)	['ʃprahrɔːr]

patrol car	Polizeiwagen (m)	[poliˈtsaɪ ˈvaːgən]
siren	Sirene (f)	[ziˈrɛnə]
to turn on the siren	die Sirene einschalten	[di ziˈrɛnə 'aɪnʃaltən]
siren call	Sirenengeheul (n)	[ziˈrɛnən geˈhɔɪl]

crime scene	Tatort (m)	[taːt ˈɔrt]
witness	Zeuge (m)	['tsɔɪgə]
freedom	Freiheit (f)	['fraɪhaɪt]
accomplice	Komplize (m)	[kɔmpˈliːtsə]
to flee (vi)	verschwinden (vi)	[fɛrˈʃwindən]
trace (to leave a ~)	Spur (f)	[ʃpuːr]

121. Police. Law. Part 2

search (investigation)	Suche (f)	['zuːhə]
to look for …	suchen (vt)	['zuːhən]
suspicion	Verdacht (m)	[fɛrˈdaht]
suspicious (suspect)	verdächtig	[fɛrˈdɛhtiħ]
to stop (cause to halt)	anhalten (vt)	[anˈhaltən]
to detain (keep in custody)	verhaften (vt)	[fɛrˈhaftən]

case (lawsuit)	Fall (m), Klage (f)	[faːl], ['klaːgə]
investigation	Untersuchung (f)	[untərˈzuːhʊŋ]
detective	Detektiv (m)	[detɛkˈtiːf]
investigator	Untersuchungsrichter (m)	[untərˈzuːhʊŋs ˈrɪħtə]

hypothesis	Version (f)	[vɛr'zɪɔ:n]
motive	Motiv (n)	[mɔ'ti:f]
interrogation	Verhör (n)	[fɛr'hø:r]
to interrogate (vt)	verhören (vt)	[fɛr'hø:rən]
to question (vt)	vernehmen (vt)	[fɛr'ne:mən]
check (identity ~)	Kontrolle, Prüfung (f)	[kɔnt'rɔlə], ['pry:fʊŋ]

round-up	Razzia (f)	['ratsia]
search (~ warrant)	Durchsuchung (f)	[dʊrh'zu:hʊŋ]
chase (pursuit)	Verfolgung (f)	[fɛr'fɔlgʊŋ]
to pursue, to chase	nachjagen (vi)	[nah 'jɑ:ɡən]
to track (a criminal)	verfolgen (vt)	[fɛr'fɔlgən]

arrest	Verhaftung (f)	[fɛr'haftʊŋ]
to arrest (sb)	verhaften (vt)	[fɛr'haftən]
to catch (thief, etc.)	ertappen (vt)	[ɛr'tapən]
capture	Festnahme (f)	['fɛstna:mə]

document	Dokument (n)	[dɔkʊ'mɛnt]
proof (evidence)	Beweis (m)	['bəvaɪs]
to prove (vt)	beweisen (vt)	['bəvaɪzən]
footprint	Fußspur (f)	['fu:sʃpʊ:r]
fingerprints	Fingerabdrücke (pl)	['fiŋə apd'rykə]
piece of evidence	Beweisstück (n)	['bəvaɪsʃtyk]

alibi	Alibi (n)	['a:libi]
innocent (not guilty)	unschuldig	['unʃʊldih]
injustice	Ungerechtigkeit (f)	['uŋ ərəhtihkaɪt]
unjust, unfair (adj)	ungerecht	['uŋ ərəht]

criminal (adj)	Kriminal-	[krimi'na:l]
to confiscate (vt)	beschlagnahmen (vt)	['bəʃla:kna:mən]
drug (illegal substance)	Droge (f)	['drɔ:gə]
weapon, gun	Waffe (f)	['vafə]
to disarm (vt)	entwaffnen (vt)	[ɛnt'vafnən]
to order (command)	befehlen (vt)	['bəfe:lən]
to disappear (vi)	verschwinden (vi)	[fɛrʃ'windən]

law	Gesetz (n)	['gəzɛts]
legal, lawful (adj)	gesetzlich	['gəzɛtslih]
illegal, illicit (adj)	ungesetzlich	['uŋ ə'zɛtslih]

| responsibility (blame) | Verantwortlichkeit (f) | [fɛrant'vɔrtlih kaɪt] |
| responsible (adj) | verantwortlich | [fɛrant'vɔrtlih] |

NATURE

The Earth. Part 1

122. Outer space

cosmos	**Kosmos** (m)	['kɔsmɔs]
space (as adj)	**kosmisch, Raum-**	['kɔsmiʃ], ['raum]
outer space	**Weltraum** (m)	['vɛltraum]
world	**All** (n)	[al]
universe	**Universum** (n)	[uni'vɛ:rzum]
galaxy	**Galaxie** (f)	[galak'si:]
star	**Stern** (m)	[ʃtɐrn]
constellation	**Gestirn** (n)	['gəʃtirn]
planet	**Planet** (m)	[pla'ne:t]
satellite	**Satellit** (m)	[zatə'li:t]
meteorite	**Meteorit** (m)	[meteɔ'ri:t]
comet	**Komet** (m)	[kɔ'me:t]
asteroid	**Asteroid** (m)	[aste'rɔ:it]
orbit	**Umlaufbahn** (f)	[umlaufba:n]
to revolve (~ around the Earth)	**sich drehen**	[ziɦ 'dre:ən]
atmosphere	**Atmosphäre** (f)	[atmɔs'fɛrə]
the Sun	**Sonne** (f)	['zɔnə]
solar system	**Sonnensystem** (n)	['zɔnən zys'te:m]
solar eclipse	**Sonnenfinsternis** (f)	['zɔnən 'finstənis]
the Earth	**Erde** (f)	['e:rdə]
the Moon	**Mond** (m)	[mɔnt]
Mars	**Mars** (m)	[mars]
Venus	**Venus** (f)	['we:nʊs]
Jupiter	**Jupiter** (m)	['ju:pitə]
Saturn	**Saturn** (m)	[za'tʊrn]
Mercury	**Merkur** (m)	[mɛr'kʊ:r]
Uranus	**Uran** (m)	[u'ra:n]
Neptune	**Neptun** (m)	[nɛp'tʊ:n]
Pluto	**Pluto** (m)	['pluto]
Milky Way	**Milchstraße** (f)	['milɦʃt'rasə]
Great Bear	**Der Große Bär**	[də 'grɔ:sə bɛ:r]

North Star	Polarstern (m)	[pɔ'larʃtɛrn]
Martian	Marsbewohner (m)	['marsbə'voːnə]
extraterrestrial (n)	Außerirdische (m)	['ausər 'irdiʃə]
alien	außerirdisches Wesen (n)	['ausər 'irdiʃəs 'wiːzən]
flying saucer	fliegende Untertasse (f)	['fliːgəndə 'untər'tasə]

spaceship	Raumschiff (n)	['raumʃif]
space station	Raumstation (f)	['raumʃta'tsɔ:n]
blast-off	Raketenstart (m)	[ra'keːtən ʃtaːrt]

engine	Motor (m)	['moːtoːr]
nozzle	Düse (f)	['dyːzə]
fuel	Treibstoff (m)	['traɪpʃtɔf]

cockpit, flight deck	Kabine (f)	[ka'biːnə]
antenna	Antenne (f)	[an'tɛnə]
porthole	Bullauge (n)	['bʊ'laugə]
solar battery	Sonnenbatterie (f)	['zɔnən batə'riː]
spacesuit	Raumanzug (m)	['raum 'antsuːk]

| weightlessness | Schwerelosigkeit (f) | ['ʃweːrəlozih kaɪt] |
| oxygen | Sauerstoff (m) | ['zauərʃtɔf] |

| docking (in space) | Ankopplung (f) | [a'ŋkɔpluŋ] |
| to dock (vi, vt) | koppeln (vi) | ['kɔpəln] |

observatory	Observatorium (n)	[ɔbzerva'toːrium]
telescope	Teleskop (n)	[teles'koːp]
to observe (vt)	beobachten (vt)	['beobahtən]
to explore (vt)	erforschen (vt)	[ɛr'forʃn]

123. The Earth

the Earth	Erde (f)	['eːrdə]
globe (the Earth)	Erdkugel (f)	['eːrtkʊːgl]
planet	Planet (m)	[pla'neːt]

atmosphere	Atmosphäre (f)	[atmɔs'fɛrə]
geography	Geographie (f)	[geogra'fiː]
nature	Natur (f)	[na'tuːr]

globe (table ~)	Globus (m)	['gloːbʊs]
map	Landkarte (f)	['lantkartə]
atlas	Atlas (m)	['atlas]

Europe	Europa (n)	[ɔɪ'rɔpa]
Asia	Asien (n)	['aːzien]
Africa	Afrika (n)	['aːfrika]
Australia	Australien (n)	[aʊst'raːlien]
America	Amerika (n)	[a'meːrika]

| North America | **Nordamerika** (n) | ['nɔrt a'meːrika] |
| South America | **Südamerika** (n) | ['zyt a'meːrika] |

| Antarctica | **Antarktis** (f) | [an'tarktis] |
| the Arctic | **Arktis** (f) | ['arktis] |

124. Cardinal directions

north	**Norden** (m)	['nɔrdən]
to the north	**nach Norden**	[naːh 'nɔrdən]
in the north	**im Norden**	[im 'nɔrdən]
northern (adj)	**nördlich**	['nørdliħ]

south	**Süden** (m)	['zyːdən]
to the south	**nach Süden**	[naːh 'zyːdən]
in the south	**im Süden**	[im 'zyːdən]
southern (adj)	**südlich**	['zyːdliħ]

west	**Westen** (m)	['vɛstən]
to the west	**nach Westen**	[naːh 'vɛstən]
in the west	**im Westen**	[im 'vɛstən]
western (adj)	**westlich, West-**	['vɛstliħ], [vəst]

east	**Osten** (m)	['ɔstən]
to the east	**nach Osten**	[naːh 'ɔstən]
in the east	**im Osten**	[im 'ɔstən]
eastern (adj)	**östlich**	[østliħ]

125. Sea. Ocean

sea	**Meer** (n), **See** (f)	['meːə], [zeː]
ocean	**Ozean** (m)	['ɔːʦeaːn]
gulf (bay)	**Bucht** (f)	[bʊht]
straits	**Meerenge** (f)	[meːə'reŋ ə]

continent (mainland)	**Kontinent** (m)	[kɔnti'nɛnt]
island	**Insel** (f)	['inzl]
peninsula	**Halbinsel** (f)	['halp 'inzl]
archipelago	**Archipel** (m)	[arhi'peːl]

bay, cove	**Bucht** (f)	[bʊht]
harbor	**Hafen** (m)	['haːfən]
lagoon	**Lagune** (f)	[la'guːnə]
cape	**Kap** (n)	[kap]

atoll	**Atoll** (n)	[a'tɔl]
reef	**Riff** (n)	[rif]
coral	**Koralle** (f)	[kɔ'ralə]

coral reef	Korallenriff (n)	[kɔ'ralən 'rif]
deep (adj)	tief	[ti:f]
depth (deep water)	Tiefe (f)	['ti:fə]
abyss	Abgrund (m)	['apgrʊnt]
trench (e.g., Mariana ~)	Graben (m)	[gra:bn]
current, stream	Strom (m)	[ʃtrɔ:m]
to surround (bathe)	umspülen (vt)	['umʃpy:lən]
shore	Ufer (n)	['u:fə]
coast	Küste (f)	['kʏstəl]
high tide	Flut (f)	[flu:t]
low tide	Ebbe (f)	['ɛbə]
sandbank	Sandbank (f)	['zantbaŋk]
bottom	Boden (m)	['bɔ:dən]
wave	Welle (f)	['vɛlə]
crest (~ of a wave)	Wellenkamm (m)	['vɛlənkam]
froth (foam)	Schaum (m)	['ʃaum]
storm	Sturm (m)	[ʃtʊrm]
hurricane	Orkan (m)	[ɔr'ka:n]
tsunami	Tsunami (m)	[tsu'na:mi]
calm (dead ~)	Windstille (f)	['wintʃtilə]
quiet, calm (adj)	ruhig	['rʊiħ]
pole	Pol (m)	[pɔ:l]
polar (adj)	Polar-	[pɔlar]
latitude	Breite (f)	['braɪtə]
longitude	Länge (f)	['lɛŋə]
parallel	Parallele (f)	[para'le:lə]
equator	Äquator (m)	[ɛk'va:tɔ:r]
sky	Himmel (m)	['himl]
horizon	Horizont (m)	[hɔri'tsɔnt]
air	Luft (f)	[lʏft]
lighthouse	Leuchtturm (m)	['løɪħt 'tʊrm]
to dive (vi)	tauchen (vi)	['tauhn]
to sink (ab. boat)	versinken (vi)	[fɛr'ziŋkən]
treasures	Schätze (pl)	['ʃɛtsə]

126. Seas' and Oceans' names

Atlantic Ocean	Atlantischer Ozean (m)	[at'lantiʃə 'ɔ:tsea:n]
Indian Ocean	Indischer Ozean (m)	['indiʃə 'ɔ:tsea:n]
Pacific Ocean	Pazifischer Ozean (m)	[pa'tsi:fiʃə 'ɔ:tsea:n]
Arctic Ocean	Arktischer Ozean (m)	['arktiʃə 'ɔ:tsea:n]

Black Sea	Schwarzes Meer (n)	['ʃvartsəs 'meːə]
Red Sea	Rotes Meer (n)	['roːtəs 'meːə]
Yellow Sea	Gelbes Meer (n)	['gɛlbəs 'meːə]
White Sea	Weißes Meer (n)	['vaɪsəs 'meːə]

Caspian Sea	Kaspisches Meer (n)	['kaspiʃəs 'meːə]
Dead Sea	Totes Meer (n)	['toːtəs 'meːə]
Mediterranean Sea	Mittelmeer (n)	['mitl'meːə]

| Aegean Sea | Ägäisches Meer (n) | [ɛ'gɛiʃəs 'meːə] |
| Adriatic Sea | Adriatisches Meer (n) | [adri'atiʃəs 'meːə] |

Arabian Sea	Arabisches Meer (n)	[a'raːbiʃɛs 'meːə]
Sea of Japan	Japanisches Meer (n)	[ja'paːniʃəs 'meːə]
Bering Sea	Beringmeer (n)	['bɛriŋ'meːə]
South China Sea	Südchinesisches Meer (n)	[zydhi'nɛːziʃəs 'meːə]

| Coral Sea | Korallenmeer (n) | [ko'ralən 'meːə] |
| Caribbean Sea | Karibisches Meer (n) | [ka'riːbiʃəs 'meːə] |

| Barents Sea | Barentssee (f) | ['barənts'zeː] |
| Kara Sea | Karasee (f) | ['karazeː] |

North Sea	Nordsee (f)	['nortzeː]
Baltic Sea	Ostsee (f)	['ɔst zeː]
Norwegian Sea	Nordmeer (n)	['nord'meːə]

127. Mountains

mountain	Berg (m)	[bərk]
mountain range	Gebirgskette (f)	['gəbirksketə]
mountain ridge	Bergrücken (m)	['bɛrkrykən]

summit, top	Gipfel (m)	['gipfl]
peak	Spitze (f)	['ʃpitsə]
foot (of mountain)	Bergfuß (m)	['bɛrk'fʊs]
slope (mountainside)	Abhang (m)	['aphaŋ]

volcano	Vulkan (m)	[vʊl'kaːn]
active volcano	tätiger Vulkan (m)	['tɛtigə vʊl'kaːn]
dormant volcano	schlafender Vulkan (m)	['ʃlaːfəndə vʊl'kaːn]

eruption	Ausbruch (m)	['ausbrʊh]
crater	Krater (m)	['kraːtə]
magma	Magma (n)	['magma]
lava	Lava (f)	['laːva]
molten (~ lava)	glühend heiß	[gly:ənt 'haɪs]

| canyon | Cañon (m) | [kaɲ'ɔn] |
| gorge | Schlucht (f) | [ʃluht] |

crevice	Spalte (f)	['ʃpaltə]
pass, col	Gebirgspass (m)	['gəbirgpas]
plateau	Plateau (n)	[pla'to:]
cliff	Fels (m)	[fɛls]
hill	Hügel (m)	['hy:gl]

glacier	Gletscher (m)	['glɛtʃə]
waterfall	Wasserfall (m)	['vasəfal]
geyser	Geiser (m)	['gaɪzə]
lake	See (m)	[ze:]

plain	Ebene (f)	['eːbənə]
landscape	Landschaft (f)	['lantʃaft]
echo	Echo (n)	['ɛhɔ]

alpinist	Bergsteiger (m)	['bɛrkʃtaɪgə]
rock climber	Kletterer (m)	['klɛtərə]
to conquer (in climbing)	bezwingen (vt)	['bətsviŋən]
climb (an easy ~)	Aufstieg (m)	['aufʃti:k]

128. Mountains names

Alps	Alpen (pl)	['alpən]
Mont Blanc	Montblanc (m)	[mɔnb'lan]
Pyrenees	Pyrenäen (pl)	[pyre'nɛən]

Carpathians	Karpaten (pl)	[kar'patən]
Ural Mountains	Uralgebirge (n)	[u'ra:lge'birgə]
Caucasus	Kaukasus (m)	[kau'kasʊs]
Elbrus	Elbrus (m)	[ɛlb'rʊs]

Altai	Altai (m)	[al'taɪ]
Tien Shan	Tian Shan (m)	[tʲan ʃan]
Pamir Mountains	Pamir (m)	[pa'mir]
Himalayas	Himalaja (m)	[hima'laja]
Everest	Everest (m)	[ɛwe'rɛst]

| Andes | Anden (pl) | ['andən] |
| Kilimanjaro | Kilimandscharo (m) | [kiliman'dʒa:rɔ] |

129. Rivers

river	Fluss (m)	[flus]
spring (natural source)	Quelle (f)	['kvɛlə]
riverbed	Flussbett (n)	[flus bət]
basin	Stromgebiet (n)	['ʃtrɔmgəbi:t]
to flow into ...	einmünden in ...	['aɪnmyndən in]
tributary	Nebenfluss (m)	['ne:bnflus]

bank (of river)	Ufer (n)	['u:fə]
current, stream	Strom (m)	[ʃtrɔ:m]
downstream (adv)	stromabwärts	['ʃtrɔ:m 'apvɛrts]
upstream (adv)	stromaufwärts	['ʃtrɔ:m 'aufvɛrts]

inundation	Überschwemmung (f)	['ju:bərʃvɛmʊŋ]
flooding	Hochwasser (n)	['hɔhvasə]
to overflow (vi)	aus den Ufern treten	[aʊs den 'ufərn 'trɛtən]
to flood (vt)	überfluten (vt)	[ju:bərf'lu:tən]

| shallows (shoal) | Sandbank (f) | ['zantbaŋk] |
| rapids | Stromschnelle (f) | ['ʃtrɔmʃnɛlə] |

dam	Damm (m)	[dam]
canal	Kanal (m)	[ka'na:l]
artificial lake	Stausee (m)	['ʃtauze:]
sluice, lock	Schleuse (f)	['ʃlɔɪzə]

water body (pond, etc.)	Gewässer (n)	['gəvɛsə]
swamp, bog	Sumpf (m), Moor (n)	[zumpf], ['mɔ:r]
marsh	Marsch (f)	[ma:rʃ]
whirlpool	Strudel (m)	['ʃtrʊ:dl]

stream (brook)	Bach (m)	[bah]
drinking (ab. water)	Trink-	[triŋk]
fresh (~ water)	Süß-	[zy:s]

| ice | Eis (n) | [aɪs] |
| to freeze (ab. river, etc.) | zufrieren (vi) | ['tsuf'ri:rən] |

130. Rivers' names

| Seine | Seine (f) | ['zɛ:nə] |
| Loire | Loire (f) | [lɔ'a:r] |

Thames	Themse (f)	['tɛmzə]
Rhine	Rhein (m)	[raɪn]
Danube	Donau (f)	['dɔ:nau]

Volga	Wolga (f)	['vɔlga]
Don	Don (m)	[dɔn]
Lena	Lena (f)	['le:na]

Yellow River	Gelber Fluss (m)	['gɛlbə flus]
Yangtze	Jangtse (m)	[jaŋ'tsɛ]
Mekong	Mekong (m)	[me'kɔŋ]
Ganges	Ganges (m)	['gaŋəs]

| Nile River | Nil (m) | [nil] |
| Congo | Kongo (m) | ['kɔŋ ɔ] |

| Zambezi | **Sambesi** (m) | [zam'bezi] |
| Limpopo | **Limpopo** (m) | [limpɔ'pɔ] |

131. Forest

| forest | **Wald** (m) | [valt] |
| forest (as adj) | **Wald-** | [valt] |

thick forest	**Dickicht** (n)	['dikiht]
grove	**Gehölz** (n)	['gəhølts]
forest clearing	**Lichtung** (f)	['lihtʊŋ]

| thicket | **Dickicht** (n) | ['dikiht] |
| scrubland | **Gebüsch** (n) | ['gəbyʃ] |

| footpath (troddenpath) | **Fußweg** (m) | ['fuːsvək] |
| gully | **Schlucht** (f) | [ʃluht] |

tree	**Baum** (m)	['baum]
leaf	**Blatt** (n)	[blat]
leaves	**Laub** (n)	['laup]

fall of leaves	**Laubfall** (m)	['laup'fal]
to fall (ab. leaves)	**fallen** (vi)	['faːlən]
top (of the tree)	**Wipfel** (m)	['wipfl]

branch	**Zweig** (m)	[tsvaɪk]
bough	**Ast** (m)	[ast]
bud (on shrub, tree)	**Knospe** (f)	['knɔspə]
needle (of pine tree)	**Nadel** (f)	['naːdəl]
pine cone	**Zapfen** (m)	['tsapfən]

hollow (in a tree)	**Höhlung** (f)	['høːlʊŋ]
nest	**Nest** (n)	[nɛst]
burrow (animal hole)	**Höhle** (f)	['høːlə]

trunk	**Stamm** (m)	[ʃtam]
root	**Wurzel** (f)	[vʊrtsl]
bark	**Rinde** (f)	['rində]
moss	**Moos** (n)	['moːs]

to uproot (vt)	**roden** (vt)	['rɔːdən]
to chop down	**fällen** (vt)	['fɛlən]
to deforest (vt)	**abholzen** (vt)	['aphɔltsən]
tree stump	**Baumstumpf** (m)	['baumʃtʊmpf]

campfire	**Lagerfeuer** (n)	['laːgə 'fɔɪə]
forest fire	**Waldbrand** (m)	[brant]
to extinguish (vt)	**löschen** (vt)	['løʃn]
forest ranger	**Förster** (m)	['førstə]

protection	Schutz (m)	[ʃʊts]
to protect (~ nature)	beschützen (vt)	['bəʃytsən]
poacher	Wilddieb (m)	['wilt'dip]
trap (e.g., bear ~)	Falle (f)	['falə]

to pick (mushrooms)	sammeln (vt)	['zaməln]
to pick (berries)	pflücken (vt)	[pflykən]
to lose one's way	sich verirren	[ziɦ fɛ'rirən]

132. Natural resources

natural resources	Naturressourcen (pl)	[na'tuːr 'resʊːrsən]
minerals	Bodenschätze (pl)	['boːdən'ʃɛtsə]
deposits	Vorkommen (n)	['fɔːrkɔmən]
field (e.g., oilfield)	Feld (n)	[fɛlt]

to mine (extract)	gewinnen (vt)	['gəwinən]
mining (extraction)	Gewinnung (f)	['gəwinʊŋ]
ore	Erz (n)	[ɛrts]
mine (e.g., for coal)	Bergwerk (n)	['bɛrkvərk]
mine shaft, pit	Schacht (m)	[ʃaht]
miner	Bergarbeiter (m)	['bɛrk 'arbaɪtə]

| gas | Erdgas (n) | ['eːrtgaːs] |
| gas pipeline | Gasleitung (f) | [gaːs'laɪtʊŋ] |

oil (petroleum)	Erdöl (n)	['eːrt øːl]
oil pipeline	Erdölleitung (f)	['ert øː'laɪtʊŋ]
oil well	Erdölturm (m)	['eːrt øːltʊrm]
derrick	Bohrturm (m)	['bɔːrtʊrm]
tanker	Tanker (m)	['taŋkə]

sand	Sand (m)	[zant]
limestone	Kalkstein (m)	['kalkʃtaɪn]
gravel	Kies (m)	[kiːs]
peat	Torf (m)	[tɔrf]
clay	Ton (m)	[tɔn]
coal	Kohle (f)	['kɔːlə]

iron	Eisen (n)	['aɪzən]
gold	Gold (n)	[gɔlt]
silver	Silber (n)	['zilbə]
nickel	Nickel (n)	['nikl]
copper	Kupfer (n)	['kʊpfə]

zinc	Zink (n)	[tsiŋk]
manganese	Mangan (n)	[man 'aːn]
mercury	Quecksilber (n)	['kvɛkzilbə]
lead	Blei (n)	[blaɪ]
mineral	Mineral (n)	[mine'raːl]

crystal	**Kristall** (m)	[kris'tal]
marble	**Marmor** (m)	['marmɔːr]
uranium	**Uran** (n)	[u'raːn]

The Earth. Part 2

133. Weather

weather	**Wetter** (n)	['vɛtə]
weather forecast	**Wetterbericht** (m)	['vɛtərbə'rıht]
temperature	**Temperatur** (f)	[tɛmpəra'tu:ə]
thermometer	**Thermometer** (n)	[tɛrmɔ'me:tə]
barometer	**Barometer** (n)	[barɔ'me:tə]
humid (adj)	**feucht**	[fɔıht]
humidity	**Feuchtigkeit** (f)	['fɔıhtıɧkaıt]
heat (extreme ~)	**Hitze** (f)	['hıtsə]
hot (torrid)	**glutheiß**	['glythaıs]
it's hot	**ist heiß**	[ist haıs]
it's warm	**ist warm**	[ist varm]
warm (moderately hot)	**warm**	[varm]
it's cold	**ist kalt**	[ist kalt]
cold (adj)	**kalt**	[kalt]
sun	**Sonne** (f)	['zɔnə]
to shine (vi)	**scheinen** (vi)	['ʃaınən]
sunny (day)	**sonnig**	['zɔnıɧ]
to come up (vi)	**aufgehen** (vi)	['aufge:ən]
to set (vi)	**untergehen** (vi)	['untərge:ən]
cloud	**Wolke** (f)	['vɔlkə]
cloudy (adj)	**bewölkt**	['bəwølkt]
rain cloud	**Regenwolke** (f)	['re:gən'vɔlkə]
somber (gloomy)	**trüb**	['try:b]
rain	**Regen** (m)	['re:gən]
it's raining	**Es regnet**	[ɛs 'rɛgnət]
rainy (day)	**regnerisch**	['re:gnərıʃ]
to drizzle (vi)	**nieseln** (vi)	['ni:zəln]
pouring rain	**strömender Regen** (m)	['ʃtrøməndə 'regən]
downpour	**Regenschauer** (m)	['re:gən'ʃauə]
heavy (e.g., ~ rain)	**stark**	[ʃtark]
puddle	**Pfütze** (f)	['pfytsə]
to get wet (in rain)	**nass werden** (vi)	[nas 'we:rdən]
fog (mist)	**Nebel** (m)	['ne:bl]
foggy	**nebelig**	['neblıɧ]

| snow | Schnee (m) | ['ʃne:] |
| it's snowing | Es schneit | [ɛs 'ʃnaɪt] |

134. Severe weather. Natural disasters

thunderstorm	Gewitter (n)	['gəwitə]
lightning (~ strike)	Blitz (m)	[blits]
to flash (vi)	blitzen (vi)	['blitsən]

thunder	Donner (m)	['dɔnɐ]
to thunder (vi)	donnern (vi)	['dɔnərn]
it's thundering	Es donnert	[ɛs 'dɔnərt]

| hail | Hagel (m) | ['ha:gl] |
| it's hailing | Es hagelt | [ɛs 'ha:gəlt] |

| to flood (vt) | überfluten (vt) | [ju:bərf'lu:tən] |
| flood, inundation | Überschwemmung (f) | ['ju:bərʃvɛmʊŋ] |

earthquake	Erdbeben (n)	['e:rtbe:bn]
tremor, quake	Erschütterung (f)	[ɛr'ʃytərʊŋ]
epicenter	Epizentrum (n)	[ɛpi'tsɛntrʊm]

| eruption | Ausbruch (m) | ['ausbrʊh] |
| lava | Lava (f) | ['la:va] |

twister	Wirbelsturm (m)	['wirbəʃʃtʊrm]
tornado	Tornado (m)	[tɔr'na:dɔ]
typhoon	Taifun (m)	[taɪ'fʊ:n]

hurricane	Orkan (m)	[ɔr'ka:n]
storm	Sturm (m)	[ʃtʊrm]
tsunami	Tsunami (m)	[tsu'na:mi]

cyclone	Zyklon (m)	[tsyk'lɔ:n]
bad weather	Unwetter (n)	['unvətə]
fire (accident)	Brand (m)	[brant]
disaster	Katastrophe (f)	[katast'rɔ:fə]
meteorite	Meteorit (m)	[meteɔ'ri:t]

avalanche	Lawine (f)	[la'wi:nə]
snowslide	Schneelawine (f)	['ʃne:lawi:nə]
blizzard	Schneegestöber (n)	['ʃne:gəʃtø:bə]
snowstorm	Schneesturm (m)	['ʃne:ʃtʊrm]

Fauna

135. Mammals. Predators

predator	Raubtier (n)	['raupti:ə]
tiger	Tiger (m)	['ti:gə]
lion	Löwe (m)	['lø:və]
wolf	Wolf (m)	[vɔlf]
fox	Fuchs (m)	[fʊks]

jaguar	Jaguar (m)	['ja:gʊa:r]
leopard	Leopard (m)	[leɔ'part]
cheetah	Gepard (m)	[ge'part]

black panther	Panther (m)	['pantə]
puma	Puma (m)	['pʊ:ma]
snow leopard	Schneeleopard (m)	['ʃnɛ:leɔpart]
lynx	Luchs (m)	[lyks]

coyote	Kojote (m)	[kɔ'jɔ:tə]
jackal	Schakal (m)	[ʃa'ka:l]
hyena	Hyäne (f)	[hy'ɛnə]

136. Wild animals

animal	Tier (n)	[ti:ə]
beast (animal)	Bestie (f)	['bɛstiə]

squirrel	Eichhörnchen (n)	['aɪhørnhən]
hedgehog	Igel (m)	[i:gl]
hare	Hase (m)	['ha:zə]
rabbit	Kaninchen (n)	[ka'ninhən]

badger	Dachs (m)	[daks]
raccoon	Waschbär (m)	['vaʃbe:r]
hamster	Hamster (m)	['hamstə]
marmot	Murmeltier (n)	['mʊrməl'ti:ə]

mole	Maulwurf (m)	['maulvʊrf]
mouse	Maus (f)	['maus]
rat	Ratte (f)	['ra:tə]
bat	Fledermaus (f)	['fle:dərmaus]
ermine	Hermelin (n)	[hɛrmə'li:n]
sable	Zobel (m)	['tsɔ:bl]

marten	Marder (m)	['mardə]
weasel	Wiesel (n)	['wi:zl]
mink	Nerz (m)	[nɛrts]

| beaver | Biber (m) | ['bi:bə] |
| otter | Fischotter (m) | [fi'ʃotə] |

horse	Pferd (n)	[pfe:rt]
moose	Elch (m)	[ɛlh]
deer	Hirsch (m)	[hirʃ]
camel	Kamel (n)	[ka'me:l]

bison	Bison (m)	[bi'zɔ:n]
aurochs	Wisent (m)	['wizɛnt]
buffalo	Büffel (m)	['byfl]

zebra	Zebra (n)	['tse:bra]
antelope	Antilope (f)	[anti'lɔ:pə]
roe deer	Reh (n)	['re:]
fallow deer	Damhirsch (m)	['damhirʃ]
chamois	Gämse (f)	['gɛmzə]
wild boar	Wildschwein (n)	['wiltʃvaɪn]

whale	Wal (m)	[val]
seal	Seehund (m)	['ze:hʊnt]
walrus	Walroß (n)	['valrɔs]
fur seal	Bärenrobbe (f)	['bɛrən'rɔ:bə]
dolphin	Delfin (m)	[dɛl'fi:n]

bear	Bär (m)	[bɛ:r]
polar bear	Eisbär (m)	['aɪsbɛ:r]
panda	Panda (m)	['panda]

monkey	Affe (m)	['afə]
chimpanzee	Schimpanse (m)	[ʃim'panzə]
orangutan	Orang-Utan (m)	[ɔ:'raŋ 'u:tan]
gorilla	Gorilla (m)	[gɔ'rila]
macaque	Makak (m)	[ma'kak]
gibbon	Gibbon (m)	[gi'bɔ:n]

elephant	Elefant (m)	[ɛle'fant]
rhinoceros	Nashorn (n)	['na:shɔrn]
giraffe	Giraffe (f)	[gi'rafə]
hippopotamus	Flusspferd (n)	['flus 'pfe:rt]

| kangaroo | Känguru (n) | ['kɛŋ urʊ] |
| koala (bear) | Koala (m) | [kɔ'ala] |

mongoose	Manguste (f)	['maŋustə]
chinchilla	Chinchilla (f)	[tʃin'tʃila]
skunk	Skunk (m)	[skʊŋk]
porcupine	Stachelschwein (n)	['ʃtahelʃvaɪn]

137. Domestic animals

cat	**Katze** (f)	['katsə]
tomcat	**Kater** (m)	['katə]
dog	**Hund** (m)	[hʊnt]
horse	**Pferd** (n)	[pfeːrt]
stallion	**Hengst** (m)	['hɛŋst]
mare	**Stute** (f)	['ʃtuːtə]
cow	**Kuh** (f)	[kʊː]
bull	**Stier** (m)	[ʃtiːr]
ox	**Ochse** (m)	['ɔksə]
sheep	**Schaf** (n)	[ʃaf]
ram	**Hammel** (m)	['haml]
goat	**Ziege** (f)	['tsiːgə]
billy goat, he-goat	**Ziegenbock** (m)	['tsiːgənbɔk]
donkey	**Esel** (m)	['ɛzl]
mule	**Maultier** (n)	['maultiːə]
pig	**Schwein** (n)	[ʃvaɪn]
piglet	**Ferkel** (n)	['fɛrkl]
rabbit	**Kaninchen** (n)	[ka'ninhən]
hen (chicken)	**Huhn** (n)	[hʊːn]
rooster	**Hahn** (m)	[haːn]
duck	**Ente** (f)	['ɛntə]
drake	**Enterich** (m)	['ɛntəriħ]
goose	**Gans** (f)	[gans]
tom turkey	**Puter** (m)	['puːtə]
turkey (hen)	**Pute** (f)	['puːtə]
domestic animals	**Haustiere** (pl)	['hausti:rə]
tame (e.g., ~ hamster)	**zahm**	[tsam]
to tame (vt)	**zähmen** (vt)	['tsɛːmən]
to breed (vt)	**züchten** (vt)	['tsyħtən]
farm	**Farm** (f)	[farm]
poultry	**Geflügel** (n)	['gəflyːgl]
cattle	**Vieh** (n)	[fiː]
herd (cattle)	**Herde** (f)	['heːrdə]
stable	**Pferdestall** (m)	['pfeːrdə 'ʃtal]
pigsty	**Schweinestall** (m)	['ʃvaɪnəʃtal]
cowshed	**Kuhstall** (m)	['kʊːʃtal]
rabbit hutch	**Kaninchenstall** (m)	[ka'ninhən ʃtal]
hen house	**Hühnerstall** (m)	['hyːnərʃtal]

138. Birds

bird	Vogel (m)	['fɔːgl]
pigeon	Taube (f)	['taubə]
sparrow	Spatz (m)	[ʃpats]
tit	Meise (f)	['maɪzə]
magpie	Elster (f)	['ɛlstə]

raven	Rabe (m)	['raːbə]
crow	Krähe (f)	['krɛːə]
jackdaw	Dohle (f)	['doːlə]
ниви	Saatkrähe (f)	['zaːtkˈrɛə]

duck	Ente (f)	['ɛntə]
goose	Gans (f)	[gans]
pheasant	Fasan (m)	[faˈzaːn]

eagle	Adler (m)	['adlə]
hawk	Habicht (m)	['haːbiħt]
falcon	Falke (m)	['falkə]
vulture	Greif (m)	['graɪf]
condor (Andean ~)	Kondor (m)	['kɔndɔːr]

swan	Schwan (m)	[ʃvan]
crane	Kranich (m)	['kraniħ]
stork	Storch (m)	[ʃtɔrh]

parrot	Papagei (m)	[papaˈgaɪ]
hummingbird	Kolibri (m)	[kɔˈlibri]
peacock	Pfau (m)	['pfau]

ostrich	Strauß (m)	['ʃtraus]
heron	Reiher (m)	['raɪə]
flamingo	Flamingo (m)	[flaˈmiŋ ɔ]
pelican	Pelikan (m)	['peːlikaːn]

| nightingale | Nachtigall (f) | ['nahtigal] |
| swallow | Schwalbe (f) | ['ʃvalbə] |

thrush	Drossel (f)	['drɔsl]
song thrush	Singdrossel (f)	[ziŋdˈrɔsl]
blackbird	Amsel (f)	['amzəl]

swift	Segler (m)	['zeːglə]
lark	Lerche (f)	['lɛrhə]
quail	Wachtel (f)	['vahtl]

woodpecker	Specht (m)	[ʃpɛħt]
cuckoo	Kuckuck (m)	[kʊˈkʊk]
owl	Eule (f)	['ɔɪlə]
eagle owl	Uhu (m)	['uːhʊ]

wood grouse	**Auerhahn** (m)	['auərhaːn]
black grouse	**Birkhahn** (m)	['biːrkhan]
partridge	**Rebhuhn** (n)	['reːphʊːn]

starling	**Star** (m)	[ʃtaːr]
canary	**Kanarienvogel** (m)	[kaˈnaːriən foɡl]
hazel grouse	**Haselhuhn** (n)	['haːzəlhʊn]
chaffinch	**Buchfink** (m)	['bʊhfiŋk]
bullfinch	**Gimpel** (m)	['gimpl]

seagull	**Möwe** (f)	['møːvə]
albatross	**Albatros** (m)	['albatrɔs]
penguin	**Pinguin** (m)	['piŋ wiːn]

139. Fish. Marine animals

bream	**Brachse** (f)	['braksə]
carp	**Karpfen** (m)	['karpfən]
perch	**Barsch** (m)	[barʃ]
catfish	**Wels** (m)	[vəls]
pike	**Hecht** (m)	[hɛɦt]

| salmon | **Lachs** (m) | [laks] |
| sturgeon | **Stör** (m) | ['ʃtøːr] |

herring	**Hering** (m)	['heːriŋ]
Atlantic salmon	**atlantische Lachs** (m)	[at'lantiʃə laks]
mackerel	**Makrele** (f)	[mak'rɛlə]
flatfish	**Scholle** (f)	['ʃɔlə]

zander, pike perch	**Zander** (m)	['tsandə]
cod	**Dorsch** (m)	[dɔrʃ]
tuna	**Tunfisch** (m)	['tʊn'fiʃ]
trout	**Forelle** (f)	[fɔ'rɛːlə]

eel	**Aal** (m)	[aːl]
electric ray	**Zitterrochen** (m)	['tsitər'rɔhn]
moray eel	**Muräne** (f)	[mʊ'rɛnə]
piranha	**Piranha** (m)	[piˈraɲja]

shark	**Hai** (m)	[haɪ]
dolphin	**Delfin** (m)	[dɛl'fiːn]
whale	**Wal** (m)	[val]

crab	**Krabbe** (f)	['krabə]
jellyfish	**Meduse** (f)	[me'dʊːzə]
octopus	**Krake** (m)	['kraːkə]

| starfish | **Seestern** (m) | ['zeːʃtərn] |
| sea urchin | **Seeigel** (m) | ['zeː'igl] |

seahorse	Seepferdchen (n)	['ze:p'fe:rthən]
oyster	Auster (f)	['austə]
shrimp	Garnele (f)	[gar'nɛlə]
lobster	Hummer (m)	['hʊmə]
spiny lobster	Languste (f)	[laŋ 'ustə]

140. Amphibians. Reptiles

snake	Schlange (f)	['ʃlaŋə]
venomous (snake)	Gift-, giftig	[ʊᵻfᵻ], ['gɪftᵻh]
viper	Viper (f)	['wi:pə]
cobra	Kobra (f)	['kɔbra]
python	Python (m)	['py:tɔn]
boa	Boa (f)	[bɔ:'a]
grass snake	Ringelnatter (f)	['riŋəl'natə]
rattle snake	Klapperschlange (f)	['klapə 'ʃlaŋə]
anaconda	Anakonda (f)	[ana'kɔnda]
lizard	Eidechse (f)	['aɪdəksə]
iguana	Leguan (m)	[legʊ'an]
monitor lizard	Waran (m)	[va'ra:n]
salamander	Salamander (m)	[zala'mandə]
chameleon	Chamäleon (n)	[ka'mɛ:leɔn]
scorpion	Skorpion (m)	['skɔrpiɔn]
turtle	Schildkröte (f)	['ʃiltkrø:tə]
frog	Frosch (m)	[frɔʃ]
toad	Kröte (f)	['krø:tə]
crocodile	Krokodil (n)	[krɔkɔ'di:l]

141. Insects

insect, bug	Insekt (n)	[in'zɛkt]
butterfly	Schmetterling (m)	['ʃmɛtərliŋ]
ant	Ameise (f)	[a'maɪzə]
fly	Fliege (f)	['fli:gə]
mosquito	Mücke (f)	['mykə]
beetle	Käfer (m)	['kɛfə]
wasp	Wespe (f)	['vɛspə]
bee	Biene (f)	['bi:nə]
bumblebee	Hummel (f)	['hʊml]
gadfly	Bremse (f)	['brɛmzə]
spider	Spinne (f)	['ʃpinə]
spider's web	Spinnennetz (n)	['ʃpinən 'nɛts]

dragonfly	**Libelle** (f)	[liˈbɛlə]
grasshopper	**Grashüpfer** (m)	[ˈgraːshypfə]
moth (night butterfly)	**Schmetterling** (m)	[ˈʃmɛtərliŋ]

cockroach	**Schabe** (f)	[ˈʃaːbə]
tick	**Zecke** (f)	[ˈtsɛkə]
flea	**Floh** (m)	[floː]
midge	**Kriebelmücke** (f)	[kriːbəlˈmyːkə]

locust	**Heuschrecke** (f)	[ˈhɔɪʃrɛkə]
snail	**Schnecke** (f)	[ˈʃnɛkə]
cricket	**Heimchen** (n)	[ˈhaɪmhən]
lightning bug	**Leuchtkäfer** (m)	[ˈløɪht ˈkɛːfə]
ladybug	**Marienkäfer** (m)	[maˈriən ˈkɛfə]
cockchafer	**Maikäfer** (m)	[ˈmaɪˈkɛfə]

leech	**Blutegel** (m)	[ˈbluːt ˈɛgl]
caterpillar	**Raupe** (f)	[ˈraupə]
earthworm	**Wurm** (m)	[vʊrm]
larva	**Larve** (f)	[ˈlarvə]

Flora

142. Trees

tree	**Baum** (m)	['baum]
deciduous (adj)	**Laub-**	['laup]
coniferous (adj)	**Nadel-**	['naːdəl]
evergreen (adj)	**immergrün**	['ımərɡryn]
apple tree	**Apfelbaum** (m)	['apfəl 'baum]
pear tree	**Birnbaum** (m)	['bɪrn'baum]
sweet cherry tree	**Süßkirschbaum** (m)	[syːsˈkɪrʃbaum]
sour cherry tree	**Sauerkirschbaum** (m)	[zauəˈkɪrʃ 'baum]
plum tree	**Pflaumenbaum** (m)	['pflaumən 'baum]
birch	**Birke** (f)	['bɪrkə]
oak	**Eiche** (f)	['aɪhə]
linden tree	**Linde** (f)	['lɪndə]
aspen	**Espe** (f)	['ɛspə]
maple	**Ahorn** (m)	['aːhɔrn]
spruce	**Fichte** (f)	['fɪhtə]
pine	**Kiefer** (f)	['kiːfə]
larch	**Lärche** (f)	['lɛrhə]
fir tree	**Tanne** (f)	['tanə]
cedar	**Zeder** (f)	['tseːdə]
poplar	**Pappel** (f)	['papl]
rowan	**Vogelbeerbaum** (m)	['foːɡəlbeːr'baum]
willow	**Weide** (f)	['vaɪdə]
alder	**Erle** (f)	['ɛrlə]
beech	**Buche** (f)	['buhə]
elm	**Ulme** (f)	['ulmə]
ash (tree)	**Esche** (f)	['ɛʃə]
chestnut	**Kastanie** (f)	[kasˈtaːniə]
magnolia	**Magnolie** (f)	[maɡˈnɔːliə]
palm tree	**Palme** (f)	['palmə]
cypress	**Zypresse** (f)	[tsypˈrɛsə]
mangrove	**Mangobaum** (m)	['maŋ ɔ'baum]
baobab	**Baobab** (m)	[baɔ'bap]
eucalyptus	**Eukalyptus** (m)	[ɔɪkaˈlyptʊs]
sequoia	**Mammutbaum** (m)	['mamʊt'baum]

143. Shrubs

bush	**Strauch** (m)	[ˈʃtrauh]
shrub	**Gebüsch** (n)	[ˈgəbyʃ]
grapevine	**Weinstock** (m)	[ˈvaɪnʃtɔk]
vineyard	**Weinberg** (m)	[ˈvaɪnbərk]
raspberry bush	**Himbeerstrauch** (m)	[ˈhimˈbeːrʃtˈrauh]
redcurrant bush	**rote Johannisbeere** (f)	[ˈrɔːtə jɔˈhanisˈbeːrə]
gooseberry bush	**Stachelbeerstrauch** (m)	[ˈʃtahelbeːrʃtrauh]
acacia	**Akazie** (f)	[aˈkaːtsiə]
barberry	**Berberitze** (f)	[ˈbərbəritsə]
jasmine	**Jasmin** (m)	[jasˈmiːn]
juniper	**Wacholder** (m)	[vaˈhɔldə]
rosebush	**Rosenstrauch** (m)	[ˈrɔːzənʃtˈrauh]
dog rose	**Heckenrose** (f)	[ˈhɛkənˈrɔːzə]

144. Fruits. Berries

fruit	**Frucht** (f)	[frʊht]
fruits	**Früchte** (pl)	[ˈfryhtə]
apple	**Apfel** (m)	[ˈapfl]
pear	**Birne** (f)	[ˈbirnə]
plum	**Pflaume** (f)	[ˈpflaumə]
strawberry	**Erdbeere** (f)	[ˈeːrtˈbeːrə]
sour cherry	**Sauerkirsche** (f)	[ˈzauəˈkirʃə]
sweet cherry	**Herzkirsche** (f)	[hɛrtsˈkirʃə]
grape	**Weintrauben** (pl)	[ˈvaɪntraubn]
raspberry	**Himbeere** (f)	[ˈhimbeːrə]
blackcurrant	**schwarze Johannisbeere** (f)	[ˈʃvartsə jɔhanisbeːrə]
redcurrant	**rote Johannisbeere** (f)	[ˈrɔːtə jɔˈhanisˈbeːrə]
gooseberry	**Stachelbeere** (f)	[ˈʃtahelbeːrə]
cranberry	**Moosbeere** (f)	[ˈmɔːsˈbeːrə]
orange	**Apfelsine** (f)	[apfelˈziːnə]
mandarin	**Mandarine** (f)	[mandaˈriːnə]
pineapple	**Ananas** (f)	[ˈananas]
banana	**Banane** (f)	[baˈnaːnə]
date	**Dattel** (f)	[ˈdatl]
lemon	**Zitrone** (f)	[ʦitˈrɔːnə]
apricot	**Aprikose** (f)	[apriˈkɔːzə]
peach	**Pfirsich** (m)	[ˈpfirziʃ]

| kiwi | Kiwi (f) | ['kiːwi] |
| grapefruit | Grapefruit (f) | ['grɛɪpfruːt] |

berry	Beere (f)	['beːrə]
berries	Beeren (pl)	['beːrən]
cowberry	Preiselbeere (f)	['praɪzəlbeːrə]
field strawberry	Walderdbeere (f)	[valt ɛrt'beːrə]
bilberry	Heidelbeere (f)	['haɪdlbeːrə]

145. Flowers. Plants

| flower | Blume (f) | ['bluːmə] |
| bouquet (of flowers) | Blumenstrauß (m) | ['bluːmənʃtraus] |

rose (flower)	Rose (f)	['roːzə]
tulip	Tulpe (f)	['tʊlpə]
carnation	Nelke (f)	['nɛlkə]
gladiolus	Gladiole (f)	[gladi'ɔːlə]

cornflower	Kornblume (f)	['kɔrnbluːmə]
bluebell	Glockenblume (f)	['glɔkən bluːmə]
dandelion	Löwenzahn (m)	['løːvɛntsaːn]
camomile	Kamille (f)	[ka'milə]

aloe	Aloe (f)	[a'loːə]
cactus	Kaktus (m)	['kaktʊs]
rubber plant, ficus	Gummibaum (m)	['gʊmi'baum]

lily	Lilie (f)	['liːliə]
geranium	Geranie (f)	['geraniə]
hyacinth	Hyazinthe (f)	[hya'tsintə]

mimosa	Mimose (f)	[mi'mɔːzə]
narcissus	Narzisse (f)	[nar'tsisə]
nasturtium	Kapuzinerkresse (f)	[kapʊ'tsiːnərk'rɛsə]

orchid	Orchidee (f)	[ɔrhi'deːə]
peony	Pfingstrose (f)	['pfiŋstrɔːzə]
violet	Veilchen (n)	['faɪlhən]

pansy	Stiefmütterchen (n)	['ʃtifmytərhən]
forget-me-not	Vergissmeinnicht (n)	[fɛr'gis'maɪ'ɲiht]
daisy	Gänseblümchen (n)	['gɛnzəb'lymhən]

poppy	Mohn (m)	[mɔːn]
hemp	Hanf (m)	[hanf]
mint	Minze (f)	['mintsə]

| lily of the valley | Maiglöckchen (n) | ['maɪgløkhən] |
| snowdrop | Schneeglöckchen (n) | ['ʃneːglɔkhən] |

nettle	Brennnessel (f)	['brɛn nɛsl]
sorrel	Sauerampfer (m)	['zauər 'ampfə]
water lily	Seerose (f)	['ze:rɔ:zə]
fern	Farn (m)	[farn]
lichen	Flechte (f)	['flɛħtə]

tropical greenhouse	Gewächshaus (n)	['gəvɛkshaus]
grass lawn	Rasen (m)	['ra:zən]
flowerbed	Beet (n)	['be:t]

plant	Pflanze (f)	['pflantsə]
grass, herb	Gras (n)	[gra:s]
blade of grass	Grashalm (m)	['gra:shalm]

leaf	Blatt (n)	[blat]
petal	Kelchblatt (n)	['kɛlħblat]
stem	Stiel (m)	[ʃti:l]
tuber	Knolle (f)	['knɔlə]

| young plant (shoot) | Jungpflanze (f) | [juŋpf'lantsə] |
| thorn | Dorn (m) | [dɔrn] |

to blossom (vi)	blühen (vi)	['blyən]
to fade, to wither	welken (vi)	['vɛlkən]
smell (odor)	Geruch (m)	['gərʊh]
to cut (flowers)	abschneiden (vt)	['apʃnaɪdən]
to pick (a flower)	pflücken (vt)	[pflykən]

146. Cereals, grains

grain	Getreide (n)	['gətraɪdə]
cereal crops	Getreidepflanzen (pl)	['gətraɪdəpflantsən]
ear (of barley, etc.)	Ähre (f)	['ɛrə]

wheat	Weizen (m)	['vaɪtsən]
rye	Roggen (m)	['rɔgən]
oats	Hafer (m)	['ha:fə]

| millet | Hirse (f) | ['hirzə] |
| barley | Gerste (f) | ['gɛrstə] |

corn	Mais (m)	['maɪs]
rice	Reis (m)	[raɪs]
buckwheat	Buchweizen (m)	['bʊhvaɪtsən]

pea plant	Erbse (f)	['ɛrpsə]
kidney bean	weiße Bohnen (pl)	['vaɪsə 'bɔ:nən]
soy	Sojabohne (f)	['zɔjabɔ:nə]
lentil	Linse (f)	['linzə]
beans (pulse crops)	Bohnen (pl)	['bɔ:nən]

COUNTRIES. NATIONALITIES

147. Western Europe

Europe	**Europa** (n)	[ɔɪˈrɔpa]
European Union	**Europäische Union** (f)	[ɔɪrɔˈpɛːɪʃə ʊˈɪiːˈjn]
Austria	**Österreich**	[øːˈstəraɪh]
Great Britain	**Großbritannien**	[grɔsbriˈtaniən]
England	**England**	[ˈɛŋlant]
Belgium	**Belgien**	[ˈbeːlɡiən]
Germany	**Deutschland**	[ˈdɔɪtʃlant]
Netherlands	**Niederlande** (f)	[nidərˈlandə]
Holland	**Holland** (n)	[ˈhɔlant]
Greece	**Griechenland**	[ˈɡriːhenlant]
Denmark	**Dänemark**	[ˈdɛnəmark]
Ireland	**Irland**	[ˈirlant]
Iceland	**Island**	[ˈislant]
Spain	**Spanien**	[ˈʃpaːniən]
Italy	**Italien**	[iˈtaliən]
Cyprus	**Zypern**	[ˈtsyːpərn]
Malta	**Malta**	[ˈmalta]
Norway	**Norwegen**	[ˈnɔrweːɡən]
Portugal	**Portugal**	[ˈpɔrtʊɡal]
Finland	**Finnland**	[ˈfinlant]
France	**Frankreich**	[ˈfraŋkraɪh]
Sweden	**Schweden**	[ˈʃweːdən]
Switzerland	**Schweiz** (f)	[ʃvaɪts]
Scotland	**Schottland**	[ˈʃɔtlant]
Vatican	**Vatikan** (m)	[vatiˈkan]
Liechtenstein	**Liechtenstein**	[ˈlihtɛnʃtaɪn]
Luxembourg	**Luxemburg**	[ˈlyksəmbʊrk]
Monaco	**Monaco**	[mɔˈnakɔ]

148. Central and Eastern Europe

Albania	**Albanien**	[alˈbaːniən]
Bulgaria	**Bulgarien**	[bʊlˈɡaːriən]
Hungary	**Ungarn**	[ˈuŋ arn]

Latvia	**Lettland**	['lɛtlant]
Lithuania	**Litauen**	['litauən]
Poland	**Polen**	['poːlən]

Romania	**Rumänien**	[rʊ'mɛniən]
Serbia	**Serbien**	['zɛrbiən]
Slovakia	**Slowakei** (f)	[slɔ'va'kaɪ]

Croatia	**Kroatien**	[krɔ'aːtsiən]
Czech Republic	**Tschechien**	['tʃehiən]
Estonia	**Estland**	['ɛstlant]

Bosnia-Herzegovina	**Bosnien und Herzegowina**	['bɔsniən unt hərtsegɔ'wina]
Macedonia	**Makedonien**	[make'dɔniən]
Slovenia	**Slowenien**	[slɔ'vɛniən]
Montenegro	**Montenegro**	[monte'nɛgrɔ]

149. Former USSR countries

| Azerbaijan | **Aserbaidschan** | [azerbaɪ'dʒan] |
| Armenia | **Armenien** | [ar'meːniən] |

Belarus	**Weißrussland**	['vaɪsrʊslant]
Georgia	**Georgien**	[ge'ɔrgiən]
Kazakhstan	**Kasachstan**	[kazahs'tan]
Kirghizia	**Kirgisien**	[kir'giːziən]
Moldavia	**Moldawien**	[mɔl'daːwiən]

| Russia | **Russland** | ['rʊslant] |
| Ukraine | **Ukraine** (f) | [ukra'iːnə] |

Tajikistan	**Tadschikistan**	[tadʒikis'tan]
Turkmenistan	**Turkmenistan**	[tʊrk'menistan]
Uzbekistan	**Usbekistan**	[usbekis'tan]

150. Asia

Asia	**Asien**	['aːziən]
Vietnam	**Vietnam**	[vjet'nam]
India	**Indien**	['indiən]
Israel	**Israel**	['izraeːl]

China	**China**	['hiːnaː]
Lebanon	**Libanon** (m)	['liːbanɔn]
Mongolia	**Mongolei** (f)	[mɔŋ ɔ'laɪ]
Malaysia	**Malaysia**	[ma'laɪzia]
Pakistan	**Pakistan**	['paːkistaːn]

Saudi Arabia	**Saudi-Arabien**	['zaudi a'ra:biən]
Thailand	**Thailand**	['taɪlant]
Taiwan	**Taiwan**	[taɪ'va:n]
Turkey	**Türkei** (f)	[tyr'kaɪ]
Japan	**Japan**	['japan]
Afghanistan	**Afghanistan**	[afganis'tan]
Bangladesh	**Bangladesch**	[baŋ la'dɛʃ]
Indonesia	**Indonesien**	[indɔ'ne:ziən]
Jordan	**Jordanien**	[jɔr'daniən]
Iraq	**Irak** (m)	[irakl]
Iran	**Iran** (m)	[iran]
Cambodia	**Kambodscha**	[kam'bɔdʒa]
Kuwait	**Kuwait**	[kʊ'vaɪt]
Laos	**Laos**	['la:ɔs]
Myanmar	**Myanmar**	[mjan'ma:r]
Nepal	**Nepal**	['ne:pal]
United Arab Emirates	**Vereinigten Arabischen Emiraten** (f)	[fɛ'raɪnihtən a'rabiʃən emi'ra:tən]
Syria	**Syrien**	['zyriən]
Palestine	**Palästina**	[palɛs'tina]
South Korea	**Südkorea**	['zy:tkɔ'rɛ:a]
North Korea	**Nordkorea**	['nɔrtkɔ'rɛa]

151. North America

United States of America	**Die Vereinigten Staaten**	[di fɛ'raɪnihtən 'ʃta:tən]
Canada	**Kanada**	['kanada]
Mexico	**Mexiko**	['mɛksikɔ:]

152. Central and South America

Argentina	**Argentinien**	[argɛn'ti:niən]
Brazil	**Brasilien**	[bra'zi:liən]
Colombia	**Kolumbien**	[kɔ'lymbiən]
Cuba	**Kuba**	['ku:ba]
Chile	**Chile**	['tʃi:lə]
Bolivia	**Bolivien**	[bo'liwiən]
Venezuela	**Venezuela**	[wenetsu'e:la]
Paraguay	**Paraguay**	[paragʊ'aɪ]
Peru	**Peru**	[pe'rʊ:]
Suriname	**Suriname**	[zuri'namə]
Uruguay	**Uruguay**	['u:rʊgvaɪ]

Ecuador	Ecuador	[ekʊa'dɔːr]
The Bahamas	Die Bahamas	[di ba'hamas]
Haiti	Haiti	[ha'iti]

Dominican Republic	Dominikanische Republik (f)	[dɔmini'kaːniʃə repʊb'liːk]
Panama	Panama	['panama]
Jamaica	Jamaika	[ja'maɪka]

153. Africa

Egypt	Ägypten	[ɛ'gyptən]
Morocco	Marokko	[ma'rɔkɔ]
Tunisia	Tunesien	[tʊ'neːziən]

Ghana	Ghana	['gana]
Zanzibar	Sansibar	[zanzi'bar]
Kenya	Kenia	['keːnia]
Libya	Libyen	['libyən]
Madagascar	Madagaskar	[mada'gaskar]

Namibia	Namibia	[na'miːbia]
Senegal	Senegal (m)	['zeːnegal]
Tanzania	Tansania	[tan'zania]
South Africa	Republik Südafrika (f)	[repʊb'liːk zyː'taːfrika]

154. Australia. Oceania

| Australia | Australien | [aʊst'raːliən] |
| New Zealand | Neuseeland | ['nɔɪzeːlant] |

| Tasmania | Tasmanien | [tas'maːniən] |
| French Polynesia | Französisch-Polynesien | [frantsøːziʃ pɔly'nɛziən] |

155. Cities

Amsterdam	Amsterdam	[amstər'dam]
Ankara	Ankara	['aŋkara]
Athens	Athen	[a'tɛn]
Baghdad	Bagdad	['bagdat]
Bangkok	Bangkok	['baŋkɔk]
Barcelona	Barcelona	[barse'løna]

| Beijing | Peking | ['pekiŋ] |
| Beirut | Beirut | [bəɪ'rʊt] |

Berlin	**Berlin**	['bɛrlin]
Bombay, Mumbai	**Bombay**	[bɔm'bɛɪ]
Bonn	**Bonn**	[bɔn]
Bordeaux	**Bordeaux**	[bɔr'dɔ]
Bratislava	**Bratislava**	[bra'tislava]
Brussels	**Brüssel**	['brysəl]
Bucharest	**Bukarest**	[buka'rest]
Budapest	**Budapest**	[buda'pɛst]
Cairo	**Kairo**	['kaɪrɔ]
Calcutta	**Kalkutta**	[kal'kuta]
Chicago	**Chicago**	[ʃi'ka:gɔ]
Copenhagen	**Kopenhagen**	[kɔpən'ha:gən]
Dar-es-Salaam	**Daressalam**	['darəszala:m]
Delhi	**Delhi**	['dɛli]
Dubai	**Dubai**	[du'baɪ]
Dublin	**Dublin**	['dublin]
Düsseldorf	**Düsseldorf**	['dysəldɔrf]
Florence	**Florenz**	[flø'rɛnts]
Frankfurt	**Frankfurt**	['fraŋkfurt]
Geneva	**Genf**	[gɛnf]
The Hague	**Den Haag**	[den ha:k]
Hamburg	**Hamburg**	['hamburk]
Hanoi	**Hanoi**	[ha'nɔɪ]
Havana	**Havanna**	[ha'vana]
Helsinki	**Helsinki**	['hɛlsiŋki]
Hiroshima	**Hiroshima**	[hirɔ'ʃima]
Hong Kong	**Hongkong**	['hɔŋkɔŋ]
Istanbul	**Istanbul**	['istanbul]
Jerusalem	**Jerusalem**	[je'ru:zalem]
Kiev	**Kiew**	['kief]
Kuala Lumpur	**Kuala Lumpur**	[ku'ala lym'pur]
Lisbon	**Lissabon**	['lisabɔn]
London	**London**	['lo:ndɔn]
Los Angeles	**Los Angeles**	['lɔs 'ɛnʤəlis]
Lyons	**Lyon**	[li'ɔn]
Madrid	**Madrid**	[mad'rit]
Marseille	**Marseille**	[mar'sɛl]
Mexico City	**Mexiko-Stadt**	['mɛksikɔ 'ʃtat]
Miami	**Miami**	[ma'jami]
Montreal	**Montreal**	[mɔnre'al]
Moscow	**Moskau**	['mɔskau]
Munich	**München**	['mynhn]
Nairobi	**Nairobi**	[naɪ'rɔ:bi]
Naples	**Neapel**	[ne'apəl]

New York	**New York**	[ɲjy: ˈjɔːk]
Nice	**Nizza**	[ˈnitsa]
Oslo	**Oslo**	[ˈɔslɔ]
Ottawa	**Ottawa**	[ɔˈtava]

Paris	**Paris**	[paˈris]
Prague	**Prag**	[prak]
Rio de Janeiro	**Rio de Janeiro**	[riːɔ de ʒaˈneːrɔ]
Rome	**Rom**	[rɔm]

Saint Petersburg	**Sankt Petersburg**	[ˈsaŋkt ˈpeːtərsbʊrk]
Seoul	**Seoul**	[zeˈuːl]
Shanghai	**Schanghai**	[ʃaŋˈhaɪ]
Singapore	**Singapur**	[ziŋaˈpʊːr]
Stockholm	**Stockholm**	[ˈʃtɔkhɔlm]
Sydney	**Sydney**	[ˈsidni]

Taipei	**Taipeh**	[ˈtaɪpeː]
Tokyo	**Tokio**	[ˈtɔkiɔ]
Toronto	**Toronto**	[tɔˈrɔntɔ]

Venice	**Venedig**	[weˈneːdiɦ]
Vienna	**Wien**	[wiːn]
Warsaw	**Warschau**	[ˈvarʃau]
Washington	**Washington**	[ˈvɔʃɪŋtən]

CPSIA information can be obtained
at www.ICGtesting.com
Printed in the USA
BVOW06s1511191117
500800BV00012B/419/P

9 781780 713199